The Next Fine Day

Elizabeth Yates

Bob Jones University Press, Greenville, South Carolina 29614

The Next Fine Day

Edited by Suzette Jordan
Cover by John Roberts
Line drawings by Nora S. Unwin

Greenville, South Carolina 29614

Printed in the United States of America

ISBN 0-89084-735-5

15 14 13 12 11 10 9 8 7 6 5 4 3 2

FOR BOB
who knows more than any of us
about the next fine day

Books for Young People by Elizabeth Yates

Amos Fortune, Free Man
Carolina's Courage
The Journeyman
Hue & Cry
Sound Friendships
Mountain Born
The Next Fine Day

Contents

The
White
Horse

Lone Flyer

1

Kent kicked a stone ahead of him on the path as he trudged the dusty distance home from school. It would have been shorter to go across the Square and through the old graveyard by St. Mary's, but he had his own reasons for not wanting to go that way.

A heron flapped overhead flying south, broad wings outspread, long thin legs trailing behind. It was a dry, warm day that felt like summer, but there were many signs that it was summer no longer. The sight of a boy walking home from school, bearing his satchel of books, was one; the pale, clean look of the harvested fields was another; and the passage of the heron. That last was unmistakable evidence that one season was over and another was at hand.

All day the herons had been livening the air over the village in their zigzag flights back and forth from the heronry in the castle grounds to their feeding places along the winding reaches of the river Stour and the nearby marshes. Gathering together at last in an open field, they had circled once more above Chilham, the castle grounds, and the tall trees in Felborough Wood that held their nests; then one by one they had soared slowly upward, long beaks and crested heads pointed south.

The year's cycle of breeding and nesting, hatching their young and caring for them until they were as at home in the air as they were stalking the riverbanks, was over. Young and old, they were leaving the fields and woods of southern England for the temperate waters and food-rich swamplands of the Mediterranean. Great wings flapped slowly, steadily as the birds went on their way. The last one, trailing far behind the others, veered in his course between village and river; his head turned slightly and his piercing eyes swept the countryside.

Kent stood still, watching the heron. "Wish I were going with you!" he called.

Nothing disturbed that steady, effortless flight. Higher and higher the heron rose, far above the line of trees and rolling hills. Sharply silhouetted against the sky, its wings flashed golden in the rays of the late afternoon sun. Kent reached down to pick up a stone, then tossed it into the air in a gesture of farewell.

"Wait! Stand just as you are, please. Only another moment."

Startled at the sound of a voice that seemed to come out of nowhere, and surprised at the request, Kent remained standing. With his eyes he could still follow the bird, small now and growing ever smaller in the remoteness of the sky. Then the heron went beyond his vision.

"Thanks, that will do nicely."

Kent turned to see who had spoken to him.

In the field just off the path, a man was sitting on a small stool. He had an easel before him with a canvas resting on it. As he talked, he busied himself putting away his painting paraphernalia.

"I've been trying all afternoon to get something into this landscape, then you and that lone heron came along at the same time."

Kent stared, wondering how he could have missed seeing the man.

"You stood watching that bird for so long that I almost had my rough sketch completed. That's why I was so peremptory when you started to move. I hope you didn't mind? What I mean is, I hope I didn't detain you too long?"

Kent shook his head.

The man began to unfasten the canvas, then he thought better and replaced it on the easel. "Perhaps you'd like to see it? Of course, it isn't finished yet, but there is something rather special about it, don't you think?"

Kent looked at the canvas, seeing on it the country he knew well—bare fields and gently rolling hills, a vastness of sky. Across the sky a single heron winged its way, so skillfully drawn that it looked as if it might fly from the canvas itself. On a near rise of land stood a boy. Only his back view could be seen and Kent would not have recognized himself had it not been for the satchel between the boy's shoulders. There was something odd about the picture. In it, the world of familiar countryside and wide-reaching sky seemed to belong as much to the boy as it did to the bird. Far apart, and soon to be even farther apart as they both were, there was something that united them.

"Nothing unusual about a heron," Kent said. "There are plenty of them around Chilham, or were until today. Nothing unusual about me either."

"Exactly," the man replied, "it's always the usual things that make the best pictures. My name is Rivven, John Rivven, artist by the grace of God and a deal of hard work. Who are you?"

"Nobody."

"Indeed? Then that's most unusual and I am glad to meet you." He closed the lid of his paint box, laid it carefully on the ground, and reached under the stool for a small wicker basket. "Won't you sit down and share my tea? The thermos holds a good two cups and my housekeeper always puts in an extra sandwich in case I meet up with anyone. Generally I do, you know, a rabbit or a horse. It's far more interesting to meet a boy."

Kent threw his book satchel on the ground and sat down beside it. "I'm not hungry."

"But one doesn't have tea because of hunger! It's a matter of sociability." John Rivven unscrewed the cap on the thermos, took out two cups nested within it, and set them on the flat surface of his paint box. He removed the cork and poured out tea.

Kent watched, then he glanced up again at the canvas on the easel. The boy began to look more like himself. He thought his mother might even recognize him, but at thought of her he wondered what she would have to say if she knew that someone had been putting him into a picture.

"Help yourself to milk and sugar." John Rivven was rummaging in the wicker basket. He placed a spoon on the paint box, then his hands went back to the basket. "There, what did I tell you! An extra sandwich, and strawberry jam at that."

"Why is it unusual to be nobody?" Kent asked.

"Because everyone must be someone by a process of relationship. He carries his father's name, or people say he looks like his mother. All that sort of thing. Links with immediate family, roots in the past, they all count in establishing identity. To be nobody would be so unusual that you might have come from the moon, which you did not."

A smile flickered over the boy's face, then went out almost as quickly as it had appeared.

"I heard what you said to the heron as it went over, and I've no doubt but that you'd like to go to the moon, if you could, or the Mediterranean."

Kent took a bite of his sandwich, then said, "I don't really belong here."

"That's interesting," John Rivven commented, as if Kent had begun to impart to him information of high value. "It has always seemed to me that we belong where we are. Of course, I agree with you that we often have to find out the reason for our being—"

"It was an accident."

"Most of us are," John Rivven said as he uncorked the thermos and refilled the two small cups. "That's what gives so many of us a common bond."

Kent looked puzzled. "It was because of an accident," he said, stressing *because,* "that my mother and I have to live here in Chilham."

John Rivven nodded thoughtfully. "I can see that you choose your words carefully. It's often the connectives that give the most trouble."

Kent opened his mouth to speak, then he closed it again. The conversation was highly peculiar, but there was nothing wrong with the jam sandwich. When the second one was offered to him, he took it without hesitation.

"It's not just being, but being in a particular place," the man went on, almost as if he were talking to himself, "like the herons. For nearly a thousand counted years and no one knows how many uncounted, they've been coming to Chilham. The trees are right for nesting, the river for feeding. So, year after year, they return, following the same air lanes, dropping down to the same nests. Of course, every year some of the young strike out to find new nesting areas, but a sufficient number return to continue their tradition."

"They've all gone now."

"Most of them. A few may stay to worry through the winter, but we won't see much of them. However, they'll all be back to herald the spring, just as they've been heralding it for probably more than a thousand years." He gazed up at the empty sky and moved his head slowly as if he never could get over the wonder, then he brought his glance down to the boy sitting beside him. "You look a little the worse for wear. How about coming back to my cottage and having a bit of a wash before you go home?"

Kent shook his head. He had almost forgotten the scrimmage he had been in on his way out of the school yard. He knew that his coat was torn in the place where his mother had mended it before; he could guess that his face was dirty and his hair rumpled. He looked at his hands. "It was a fight," he said, "and I lost."

"You didn't really need to tell me. I could see as much for myself. Well, the ancient Britons lost, too. Or did they?"

"Whatever do you mean?"

John Rivven gestured. The sweep of his arm went down to the river and up to a near hillock. "It might have been there," he said, "somewhere between the river and the rise of land on which Chilham sits, that the ancient Britons took their stand against the armed might of Caesar. They fought well, those little men with their crudely fashioned shields and bronze swords, but they were no match for the well-trained, heavily armed soldiers who came marching up from behind their strongly built fortifications.

"Wave after wave the Romans came, like a tide running full. Before them, the little men and their rude earthworks were only a minor halt. Oh, they fought bravely, those early Britons, as they sought to turn the tide, but when they could stand up no longer to the Roman legions they broke and scattered. Back across the river Stour they fled and into the woods with the Roman soldiers in pursuit. History tells us that the Britons were vanquished, but were they?"

"Of course," Kent said. He could have told Mr. Rivven the very page in the history book at school that said as much.

"The Romans won that first encounter, even though Caesar's tribune, Quintus Laberius Durus, was killed and they lost many men, though not nearly so many as were lost by the Britons. Here, in this very spot, perhaps right where we are sitting, you might say that there began the history of the England we know today."

Kent was puzzled. "But if the ancient Britons lost? They fought again, didn't they? They tried—"

"Yes, indeed, but that first battle was decisive. Oh, don't think that you have to be the victor to win in the end! The Romans pursued the Britons deep into their land and the Romans remained. In time they were absorbed into the life of Britain, as conquerors are, and—well, to sum up a very long piece of history, the herons returned in that spring of 55 B.C. to their nests along the river Stour."

"Are you sure?"

"I am sure that the sun did not fail to rise no matter what was the outcome of the clashing swords," John Rivven said. "I am equally sure that the herons did not fail to follow their long-established pattern."

Kent sighed. Just as things were beginning to make sense, Mr. Rivven brought up the herons. "Whatever have the Chilham herons got to do with the Romans and their war against the ancient Britons?"

"Everything, or nothing," came the provocative answer, "however you want to look at it. There is a saying in Chilham that if the herons return in early February, all will be well and good with the village for another year."

"And if they don't return?"

John Rivven shook his head slowly. "There has never been a year when life has not been good. The clashing of swords dies away in the distance and in its stead across the years the ear picks up other sounds—the clacking of a loom, the grinding of a mill, voices, lowings, baaings. Threading them together are the songs—some strident, some melodious—of birds.

"After winter's dark and cold, days begin to lengthen, buds begin to swell on the trees. Fish come up the river. Men go out to seed fields that have lain fallow for months. Cattle are given their freedom in greening pastures. Everything has its season, and as the wheel of the year turns, we come to see that there is a time for every purpose under heaven. Life that might have looked bleak and hard during the winter begins to look good again in spring."

Kent, listening, hoped that Mr. Rivven would not soon come to a stop; but stop he did, with a glance at the sky and a shake of his head.

"So, the last of the herons has gone over, and if I'm not mistaken we've had the last of our good weather for a while. The wind has changed as we've been sitting here. Have you far to go?"

"Not too far. The other side of the village. The road that leads to the Lees."

"Anyone expecting you?"

"My mother, but she doesn't get home from Canterbury until six o'clock."

"You've still got nearly an hour and daylight enough to see you home. You're not a man of Kent, are you?"

The boy shook his head.

"Or a Kentish man?"

Again he shook his head. Then, with an air of embattled defiance, Kent burst out, "I told you I'm nobody. Part English. Part American. I don't know where I belong. I'm not one thing or the other. That's why—" He checked his words quickly and turned away from the man whose kindly interest had made him feel contentious.

"I suppose you have a name."

"It's Kent."

"Kent?"

"Kent Conner. It was my father's name. It has nothing to do with the county of Kent."

"But perhaps it has, Kent!" John Rivven exclaimed excitedly. "Names don't just happen. They're generally given to us for some very good reason, though it may be so distant that it's all but forgotten. You say your father was an American. Where was he born?"

"In a place called Virginia. It's a state, not a city."

John Rivven waited a moment, but Kent had apparently said all that he wanted to say or all that he knew, for he hunched up his knees to rest his chin on them and was staring off across the countryside.

"Virginia," the man repeated under his breath, and then as if he were thinking out loud, "Virginia and Chilham. Long ago there was a link between those two. Perhaps the link has held right up to the present—Virginia, U.S.A., and Chilham in the county of Kent, England."

The boy had lifted his head and was looking intently at the man.

"Kent, if I'm not mistaken, you've got more than a name. You've got the glory of a county on your shoulders."

"What—what do you mean?" Curiosity struggled with embarrassment and again the smile flickered over the boy's face, but this time it did not go out entirely.

"More than I can say now or we'll both be late at our respective homes. What do you say to meeting again on the next fine day?"

"Where? Here?"

John Rivven thought for a moment, then said, "How about the castle grounds, near where the great mulberry stands? I've always wanted to make some sketches of that tree." He stood up and folded the stool, unfastened his canvas, and began to fold the easel.

"But will the lodge-keeper let me in to the castle grounds?"

"Tell her who you are. When she lets me through I'll ask her to look out for you."

Kent nodded and repeated, "The next fine day, by the great mulberry, in the castle grounds." He was country bred enough to know by the look of the sky and the feel of the wind that tomorrow would not be that day; he was sufficiently intrigued to hope that the day would not be too distant.

"Mr. Nobody indeed!" the artist said, holding out his hand and shaking Kent's. Then he picked up his gear, said a good-by, and started along the path in the direction of a small cottage that Kent had seen before but never thought much about, since it had always appeared to be empty.

Kent picked up his satchel and walked in the opposite direction toward the village. He walked slowly, companioned by great thoughts: this was the ground where the ancient Britons had taken their stand and where the Roman legions had first struck.

He stopped and looked around him, then scuffed at the earth with the toe of his boot. Reaching down, he picked up a small handful of the loosened soil and let it run from the palm of one hand to the palm of the other, then he tipped what remained into a pocket of his jacket. Kent straightened his shoulders. The earth that had once been fought over so bitterly was his earth now.

Ahead of him the clock in the flint-and-stone tower of St. Mary's was striking six. He started to run. There was no way now that he could get ahead of time, but at least he need not be quite so far behind it.

Maidey Conner, much to her surprise, had reached home before her son. She was not worried. She would save that for darkness and trust that he would return while there was still light in the sky. She hoped his lateness meant that he had found some boy to play with, or that he was doing an errand for one of the shopkeepers. She knelt down by the grate to lay the fire on the cold ashes. Whatever it was that was making him late, he would be hungry when he came in and wanting his supper. She had just placed the lamp on the table when Kent came in the door.

" 'Evening, Mum."

"You're very late, Kent."

"Sorry."

Before she could say another word, he had gone past her to the shed where the pump was and soon she heard sounds of splashing water. When he returned, his face and hands were clean and his hair was neatly smoothed down. Whatever tale his appearance might have told had been washed away; only the tear in his jacket remained.

It was the first thing that caught Maidey's eye. "You've torn your jacket!" she exclaimed.

Kent put his hand along the rent. "It was—well, it might be called an accident."

Maidey knew well enough what it was. She made a little clicking sound with her tongue. "It's been mended before and it can be mended again, but it's a new jacket you're needing, that's plain to see."

Kent assured his mother of his hunger, but when they sat down to eat he talked so constantly that she finally had to ask him to pay attention to his food before it got cold.

"I've never known you to take so much interest in history. Is it a new book you've started on at school?"

"Oh, this isn't school!" Kent exclaimed. "I met a man on my way home and we were talking together. He gave me some of his tea." Kent's left hand returned to the pocket of his jacket and Maidey wondered what he had found that he must finger it so often.

"A man," she repeated. "Well, there's no harm in that." Some farmer, she thought, or perhaps one of the gypsies who lived in caravans on the Downs. Even a tinker traveling through the countryside might have had a flask of tea in his pack. "I hope you thanked him properly."

Kent looked startled. "I—I never thought about saying thanks. We were having such an interesting time talking. I just forgot. Oh, Mum, he knows so many stories. He told me all about—"

"If you ever see him again, which you may not if he's a passing stranger, remember to say your thanks to him, even if they are out of time. And how was school today? Did you do well?"

Kent stared across the table as in his mind he reached back into the day. School, and all that had taken place from morning to midafternoon, seemed farther away than the stand of the ancient Britons. He shrugged his shoulders.

Maidey knew what the gesture meant and she felt helpless before it. Life was going to be hard for Kent, as it had been for her. Perhaps it was as well that he got used to the fact in his early years instead of filling himself with notions that it could be otherwise. And yet, as Maidey looked at him, she felt there was something about him that had not been there last night when they had sat at their supper. She could not say what it was, unless it was some hint of the man she hoped he would be and had almost despaired of ever seeing emerge.

"You'll not do well by that kipper using only your fork," she reminded him.

Kent brought his left hand out of his pocket and took up his knife, looking across the table at her with a sudden swift smile.

"That's better," she sighed. "At least you can learn to eat like a gentleman."

She kept her eyes on him. He was in so many ways like that other Kent, even to the smile that often took the place of words. Sometimes it seemed that all she had ever given him was that straight, straw-colored hair that lay so close to his head.

"The last of the herons went over today, Mum," Kent said as he laid his knife and fork across his empty plate and his left hand dropped down to his pocket. "I saw him go, clear across the sky."

"That means winter will be upon us soon. Dark days, rain and cold." Maidey shuddered with anticipation. "And hard times."

"Or does it?" Kent asked.

The Mulberry

2

The first of the autumn rains, harbinger of all that were to come, swept over the countryside before dawn. No one in Chilham had expected the good weather to last long after the herons went, but no one had expected the bad weather to come quite so soon. One rainy day followed another and when the rain finally ceased, dampness like a lid settled over the land from the Downs to the sea. Sometimes a streak of sunshine got through, but there was nothing in the succession of gray cool days that could go by the name of fine.

"The herons know when it's time to go" was the expression heard often around the village.

People missed the great birds, silent in their flying and noisy in their nests; but their coming in the spring and going in the autumn had been the pattern of life for so long that it was as accepted as routine. Any change in it would have been cause for alarm.

Kent missed them in a different way. As long as they crossed the near sky, stalked the river, or took off in farther flight beyond the Downs, he could imagine what it would be like to be one of them, to go with them wherever they were going, to some not distant marsh or to their winter feeding grounds. Without them he was trapped in a small village in which he felt he had never belonged.

"Why do we stay here?" he asked his mother repeatedly.

Her answer was always the same. "Where else would we go?" Then she explained to him all over again that the rent was cheap and her work in Canterbury was good. "At least I can be home in time every night to get your supper, Kent, and I have one day free a week for my own washing and cleaning, as well as Christmas and Bank Holidays."

The argument was unanswerable, Kent knew, but it never satisfied him. "We don't belong here," he persisted.

"I do, Kent, and so do you until your schooling's done."

Maidey Conner's life had been bounded by the Downs on the north and Canterbury on the south. A dozen years ago she had spent a week in London, and there had been occasional weekends by the sea at Walmer or Ramsgate when Kent was a baby. She had accepted her horizons without question. That Kent could not accept his was no surprise to her, but that she could do nothing to help him was her continuing bafflement.

"You'll have to wait until you're old enough to go to work, Kent, then you can choose for yourself." She might have added "perhaps," but she had no wish to make things harder for Kent than they were bound to be.

Every such conversation ended with Kent silently counting on his fingers the years that remained before he would be old enough to work.

* * *

The longed-for fine day came at last. For some it meant that washing could be hung out in the air to dry, for others that work in the fields could be resumed; for Kent it meant a promised meeting. The sun struggled through early morning haze to shine with reasonable cheer, and by midday a caressing warmth rested on the land. But though the day was fine and expectation made it even finer, things did not go well for Kent at school. He failed miserably in composition, a subject in which he generally did well.

"Think of a wish," Miss Hinshaw said, "and write about that. Take a few minutes to think before you begin to write. I shall ring the bell in one half-hour and all papers must be turned in then."

"A wish?" someone asked.

"Yes, something you would like to have." Miss Hinshaw turned to correct the arithmetic papers that were on her desk.

Silence took over, infringed upon only by the ticking of the clock, an occasional sigh, or a quick little gasp of inner excitement. One after another pencils started to move over blank sheets of ruled paper, some laboriously, some rapidly, as the members of the class met the assignment.

Kent looked out of the window, then he looked around the room at the heads bowed over desks and the hands moving pencils. He could guess what different ones were writing about. Madge had always talked about wanting to have a pony of her own. Tom was forever saying what he would do when he went to London. Kent wondered about some of the others. Tessa, whose large family lived in one of the smallest cottages on the Downs, must have plenty of things to wish for. None of them, Kent thought, would mind having their papers read aloud to the class, as Miss Hinshaw often did with compositions. For all of them, wishes were possible things.

But his—he gripped his pencil hard—nothing could make it come true. There was no use writing it down. His eyes were stinging. He put his head down on the ruled white paper on his desk.

The bell rang.

"Sign your papers and turn them in," Miss Hinshaw announced. "Class is dismissed."

Kent wrote his name and the date at the top of his paper. He took particular care and an undue amount of time in straightening the contents of his desk. When the others had left the room, he went up to the teacher's desk and placed his paper on the pile before her.

"But, Kent," she said, "you haven't done what I asked you to do."

"Nothing to wish for that I can have."

"Wishes are hopes," she reminded him.

"That doesn't matter."

"I can't mark you on this, Kent. You will have to do another paper. Tomorrow. During preparation hour."

"Not on wishes," he said stubbornly.

Miss Hinshaw could be stubborn too. "You may write on anything you like, but see that you turn in to me a paper twice as long. That means two sheets, to make up for today. And it must embrace the central idea given to the class. Now, you may go."

Even being detained at the desk could not save Kent from the scorn of his schoolmates. The boy sitting next to him had seen the empty paper and told the others about it. Several were waiting for him in the playground.

"If wishes were horses, beggars would ride," Tom sang out as Kent came through the door.

"Just like a nobody to write nothing," another boy jeered.

Kent turned up his collar as if the wind were blowing and started away from the playground. Their voices followed him.

"—'fraid, that's what he is."

"—doesn't want us to know."

"Nobody—nobody—"

The words hit his ears like a shower of well-aimed stones.

Kent had gone a considerable distance before he realized how warm it was with the sun shining and his collar turned up. He stood still for a moment and looked around him. It was a fine day all right. The country looked green after the recent rains, though very sodden. The leaves had been falling fast and many of the trees were bare. It wouldn't be long now to winter, but even winter had its fine days.

Kent turned and retraced his steps to the village. When he reached the heavy wooden gates that led to the castle, he put his hand on the iron ring and found that one of the gates yielded to his touch. He pushed it open and looked into the castle grounds. A window went up in the lodge just inside the gates. At sight of the boy standing there the keeper called out to him.

"You must be the lad Mr. Rivven told me to look out for."

"I'm Kent Conner. Is he really expecting me today?"

"He is, Kent. I let him through an hour or more ago. It's all right for you to join him. Come along in."

"Thank you. Thank you very much." Kent stepped forward and pushed the big gate behind him until it closed.

"Do you know where to find him?"

"He said he'd be by the great mulberry."

"That's in the very center of the vegetable garden. Keep to the left as you go round the potting sheds."

Kent walked quickly until he came to the place. He saw the great mulberry from a distance, but it was not the only one. A younger tree grew near, its reaching limbs propped up with thick wooden sticks, and there was a third and smaller mulberry. The old tree was supported by one huge prop; facing it the artist sat. His back was all that Kent could see, and the easel upon which a large pad rested. As Kent approached, he noticed that a wicker basket stood beside the stool. It looked larger than the one that had held the tea on their first day of meeting.

Maidey had always been particular about Kent's knocking on a door before entering a room. With this in mind, Kent did not like to approach from the rear without announcing himself in some way. He scuffed a few pebbles ahead of him in the path and waited to see what would happen.

John Rivven went on with his work. Without turning his head he said, "I thought you'd be along about now. Come and tell me what you think of it. I'm very nearly finished."

Kent stood beside his friend, studying the lines on the sketch pad.

"Like it?"

Kent nodded. It was a great tree, burled and bent, yet so rooted that it looked as if no force could ever dislodge it.

John Rivven made a few final touches, then he put his crayon back in its box. "The Chilham Castle mulberry," he announced, "grandparent, so it is said, by many greats, of all the mulberries in Virginia."

"Virginia!" Kent exclaimed. He looked more closely at the canvas, then beyond it to the actual tree—covered with burls, twisted by time, its roots reaching far down into the earth. He glanced from the real tree to the replica and back again. "You're a very good artist," he said. "Yes, I think you're a very good artist indeed."

"I'm jolly glad to hear that, especially from you."

"Me?"

"Yes, you, because I think you've had something to do with mulberry trees. Oh, not recently, but long ago. I'll tell you about it when we settle down. Aren't you ready for some tea?"

"I could be."

John Rivven opened the basket and started to take out the tea things. He spread a small cloth on the grass and placed on it various containers. "You see, I really am prepared for you today." He pointed to the two thermos bottles. "And my housekeeper made some mulberry tarts for us. She always has some fruit of the countryside preserved for special occasions."

Kent gazed at the ceremonial feast, then he sat down on the grass, took the proffered cup of tea and a tart.

"How did things go today?"

"Not very well."

"Hmm, but no fights?"

Kent shook his head. "I couldn't do the composition Miss Hinshaw gave to the class so I turned in a blank paper. I have to make up for it tomorrow."

"Lucky for me she didn't keep you on today!"

"For *you?*"

"Of course. I might have been having tea all by myself."

Kent took a long swallow and ate half a tart. Feeling better, he said, "She asked us to write about a wish and I couldn't do it."

"Nothing you want?"

"That I can have."

"I see. That does make it difficult."

Kent took a deep breath. Then he ate the other half of his tart and refilled his cup from the thermos.

John Rivven glanced up at his sketch and off at the tree. "There's still some work to do on it," he said, talking more to himself than to Kent.

The boy followed his glance. "That mulberry tree—what has it got to do with Virginia?"

"It's a long story, and a rather wonderful one." John Rivven spoke slowly as he brought the words out of memory. "That mulberry is said to be the oldest such tree in all of England. At one time there were many such trees in the castle grounds, but these are the only ones that remain."

Kent leaned forward and listened while he was told of the Digges family who had lived in Chilham Castle three hundred years ago. "Colonel Digges was made a governor of the royal colony of Virginia, by order of King James. When he set out to cross the Atlantic, he took with him cuttings from the mulberry trees in his castle grounds. Months later he established them in Virginia at a place called Mulberry Island, where they began to thrive. Their full-flavored fruit was much sought after, and their leaves were used for silkworm culture to promote a beginning industry.

"Like as not, plenty of cuttings were made from those trees once they got to growing on Mulberry Island. In fact, it's entirely possible, as the story goes, that most of the mulberry trees in

America are descended from this parent tree near which we are both sitting and having our tea."

Kent looked with renewed respect at the ancient tree, then at the one on the easel.

"If you've read your history, you'll remember that after a while there were no more royal governors in Virginia, and no royal standard flying from the palace at Williamsburg; but there were mulberry trees. Rooted deep and sure, they grew in the new land as vigorously and productively as they had grown in old England. And there were people, English men and women who had been absorbed by the new land as Caesar's soldiers were absorbed by the land they set out to conquer."

During the silence that followed John Rivven's words, Kent's thoughts were all of that place called Virginia, once remote and meaningless to him, now become near and compelling. If, when he grew up, he ever went there, he knew that he would not feel like a stranger. He would see mulberry trees there that were related to the one he was looking at now. He would be able to touch them, as he could this one. It seemed to him then that near and far, geographically as well as chronologically, were within the span of outstretched arms.

"So, your name is Kent. Tell me what you know about it."

"It was my father's name."

"And he came from Virginia?"

"Yes. It was his father's name."

"Ah"—John Rivven's face became excited, as if together they stood on the edge of a discovery—"and if you could go back, back through the years, you might find that name appearing and reappearing, sometimes as a surname, sometimes because carried by a girl as a given name. You might find that it went back to the time when Colonel Digges and his men journeyed to America with mulberry cuttings packed carefully in soil that was dampened with fresh water all through the long voyage.

"Perhaps there was among them one man, green-fingered, young, and filled with hope, who tended the mulberries on the voyage and when they were finally planted in the new world. As they took root and established themselves, grew and flourished, people came to say that the man from Kent had done that. Then the man called one of his sons Kent, in tender memory of a land he knew he'd never see again. Through the years the name was repeated, so that in one particular family there was always a Kent."

"How do you know all this?"

"I don't know exactly. I'm just having fun making up something that might be true. The history books and the books about history tell us many things, but there are many more things that you can tell yourself to fill in the gaps. Imagination is better than spectacles when it comes to picking up what's between the lines."

Kent's eyes were shining. "Do you think, do you really think, that perhaps there was a man who made mulberries grow in the new world and who named his son Kent?"

"Yes, I do. I most certainly do. It's so probable that it is very likely true. We all wear cloaks made up of tattered bits of history. Yours may be more of a piece than you think."

"I—I've never even thought—"

"Begin then, and go on."

Kent found it difficult to capture in words all that was welling up in his mind. "If it is so, then—then my being born here, living here, means I've come back, or rather my long-ago ancestor has come back in me, the one who thought he might never see the county of Kent again."

John Rivven was studying the boy's face, wishing he might catch in penciled line on paper the animation that had come into it.

Kent got up and went across the grass to the great mulberry tree. He put both hands on its knobby trunk, then looked up into the tangle of its leafless branches. He might have been placing his hands in those of a friend; he might have been looking into a friend's face.

When he came back to throw himself on the grass beside the tea basket, he sighed happily. "That year that Colonel Digges went to America with the mulberry slips and the man who was to care for them, do you think the herons returned to the Chilham heronry?"

"Yes, I do, Kent. I do, indeed, for all was well with Chilham. In fact, all was very well. Something had reached from the old world to the new, something that might never have happened if mulberries had not grown well in Chilham soil and someone believed that they would grow well in Virginian soil. An ocean—a Revolution—a hundred years, or two, or three, matter little when hope is present."

The sun had begun to haze off in the west. The artist started to pack the tea things back in the wicker basket, then he picked up his sketch pad and folded his stool and easel so he could carry everything easily.

"Might I help you?" Kent asked.

"Thanks, but I'm used to carrying my gear and we go in opposite directions. Beekeep isn't as far as your home, I'm thinking."

"Beekeep?"

"Yes, that's the name of my cottage. Before I came to live in it a few months ago it was a place where an old man kept bees. There's one hive left by the kitchen door. My housekeeper takes more care of it than I do."

When they shook hands in parting, John Rivven said, "Don't forget what's between the lines."

Kent looked puzzled.

"When you do that composition tomorrow."

Kent smiled. School, and unmarked papers, and taunting school fellows seemed very far away.

John Rivven turned and started off through the castle grounds. Kent watched him walk down the gravel path; he watched him grow smaller and smaller as he went on his way. Nothing had been said about their meeting again, but Kent had a comfortable feeling that the next fine day could not be far distant.

Before leaving, he went back to stand beside the old mulberry tree and put his hands on its bark. Now, almost more than anything else in the world, he wanted to go to Virginia and see for himself how the descendants of the Chilham trees were faring. Kent stooped over and picked up a handful of loose earth from near the base of the tree. He dribbled it from one palm to the other. As he did so, words that were not his yet came from within him moved in his mind:

Take of English earth as much
As either hand may rightly clutch—

It was as if someone had said them to him a long time ago, but who it was or when they were uttered he did not know. He poured some of the earth into his pocket and started home.

* * *

That night at supper when Kent told his mother about his second meeting with Mr. Rivven, Maidey had only one thought. "Did you remember to say your thanks to him, Kent? This will be two teas that you've had with him."

Kent shook his head.

"How can you be so forgetful?" Maidey exclaimed. "I can't give you much in this world, but I would like to feel that I had given you some proper manners."

Kent tried to explain how it was that he forgot. He told his mother about the interesting things Mr. Rivven said, things that made them both start thinking. "Besides, Mum, he knows I'm grateful to him even if I don't say so."

Maidey was firm. "There isn't any way anyone can know anything unless it's said in words."

Maybe she was right, Kent thought. After all, he would not have known a thing about the old mulberry and the man from Kent if Mr. Rivven had not put it into words.

"Mum, I promise you, really I do, that the next time I see him I'll say thank-you first thing."

"The next time? Then he does live around here?"

"Yes, up on the Downs, in Beekeep Cottage. He has a hive of bees and a housekeeper."

"That's not much to go through life with."

"He's an artist. He draws pictures."

Maidey drew in her breath. Artists were odd folk. She had heard tales enough about them. Artists and writers, they were all cut from the same piece of cloth. "I can tell you a thing or two about artists when you're older," she said, then she stood up to clear the table.

Two Compositions

3

Kent sat back in his chair, ready to listen with the rest of the class to Miss Hinshaw's reading of one of the compositions. Knowing quite well that his would not be read, he was prepared to enjoy whatever paper she had chosen. More than a week had passed since the assignment had been given out. Kent had made up for his failure by writing the double-length paper, but he had quite forgot the discipline imposed on him in the excitement of the writing.

Following his meeting with Mr. Rivven near the ancient mulberry tree, he had been filled with wondering. Everyone in Chilham knew the mulberry, as they knew St. Mary's and the Woolpack Inn, and Robin's Croft and all the other places that the tourists and visitors to the village always wanted to see; but how many knew about the cuttings from the tree that had gone to America and been planted there years and years ago? No one in all of Chilham, it was safe to say, knew how the Virginian descendants of the Chilham trees were faring. Someone would have to go there to find out.

Kent shivered with excitement at the thought that he might well be the one to go. It had not been easy to confine his thoughts to the two pages required for the composition. There was so much he wanted to go on saying.

Now he was impatient to get his paper back, no matter what mark it bore. It was like one of Mr. Rivven's sketches: there were still things he wanted to do to it.

"I have two papers to read aloud, for quite different reasons," Miss Hinshaw announced. "Each one deals with the subject given the class, one directly, the other indirectly. Both are carefully written. Frankly, because I cannot decide which one is the better, I am going to ask you to make the decision."

The class regarded her silently, awed by their responsibility.

Miss Hinshaw's reading voice was entirely different from her speaking voice. When she spoke, her words were brisk and matter-of-fact; when she read, her words sounded as if they had been set to music. She pronounced the title, "I Wish," then looked across the classroom to be sure that she had gathered everyone's attention.

Kent listened as the lilting voice took up the thoughts that had been committed to paper. He was curious to know the writer. The word *wish* was repeated often, not because the writer could not think of another word but because of its importance. Whoever had written the paper wished for skill in mending broken things.

> *It hurts me to find an injured bird and not know what to do for it. I wish I knew. I wish I could learn. Sometimes I can help, but often I only do the sort of thing that though it might be right for a person is not necessarily right for a bird. Each form of life requires some special knowledge. If I could learn the first things, I might be able some day to learn how to help mend a broken world. I wish I could always be a mender and never a breaker. But help for the world would not be in fingers but in thoughts. I wish my thoughts could grow to be as strong as the wings that bring the herons back every spring to tell us that all is well. But most of all do I wish that the "well" were not just for our village but for the world.*

Miss Hinshaw laid the paper down on her desk and made a little drumming noise with her fingers, a sound she often employed to accent a final period.

Some of the class who were sitting in positions where they could turn their heads easily looked around the room, trying to decide who had written the composition. Most of the faces were passive, except for a smile of admiration here, or a tongue moistening lips there. No one, by attitude or gesture, was giving authorship away.

Aware of the mood of listening that had been created, Miss Hinshaw picked up the second paper and began to read it. One head then another bent forward to listen more intently. This was a story about something they all knew, and yet it leaped distance to tell them about something they did not know. Kent dug his nails into his palms until his fingers ached.

> *When the life of a tree can reach across the ocean so that something of the old trunk lives on in the young shoots, a link has been made that nothing can break. Years will not mar it, even war will not sever it. If a cutting is taken from a sound tree by a man who has green fingers and a heart of hope, then placed in good soil and cared for, it will grow. This is something about which we can be sure. Once it starts to grow it will go on, bearing blossoms and in time, fruit. This happened long before the days of the ancient Britons; it will go on happening long after we are gone.*

Miss Hinshaw turned the paper and read the second page that told of Chilham's past and its present far beyond the borders of Kent where scions from its mulberry trees were flourishing. Her voice had more of a lilt to it than ever, and there was a proud lift to her head when she came to the final line, *"It is the growing that matters."*

She put the two sheets together on her desk and drummed lightly with her fingers. The period was in the right place, but she was not the only one who wished it had not come so soon. She looked into the faces before her. A dozen pair of eyes met hers. One head was turned away, its glance directed through the window toward the ancient wall that stood between the school yard and the castle grounds.

"Do you see now why I could not choose?" Miss Hinshaw asked.

Madge, so often spokesman for the class, stood up beside her desk. "Miss Hinshaw, couldn't you give each paper the high mark?"

A sudden clapping of hands in release and approval sounded through the room.

"Yes, I could do that," Miss Hinshaw said with a nod. "And now, will our two authors come forward?"

Kent wondered if his knees would hold him up, but they did, and he walked with a light swift step down to the teacher's desk. Tessa, the dark-haired girl commonly known as the gypsy because she lived near an old gypsy camp on the Downs, also approached the desk.

"Tessa, Kent, I think we're all very proud of you. You've set a new standard for us." Miss Hinshaw shook hands with Tessa, then with Kent; then the boy and girl solemnly shook hands with each other while the rest of the children clapped and banged on their desks until Miss Hinshaw called for quiet.

After the papers had been returned to the various members of the class, each paper bearing the mark the teacher felt it merited, the class was dismissed. Boys and girls poured out into the playground in haste lest they lose a moment of rightful play. Kent lingered at his desk, finding one thing and another to do until the room was empty. Then he approached Miss Hinshaw.

"I don't know how you could call my composition a wish," he said. "I never even used the word, except in the title. I just wrote about something I knew, and then because I had to do another page, about something I'd like to know."

"And isn't that wishing?"

Kent shrugged his shoulders.

"You established something certain on your first page, Kent, something that might almost be called 'mulberry culture.' Your second page comes alive with longing to see for yourself how some particular mulberry trees are thriving in a particular part of the world."

He nodded his head slowly, glad that he had met the requirement even without full awareness of having done so.

"How did you learn all this, Kent? You've told me things I've never known before, and I've no intention of questioning your truthfulness."

"It wasn't my idea in the first place, really it wasn't, Miss Hinshaw. You see—" Then he told her of the man he had met on two occasions and of the conversations they had had together.

"It might have been his thought at first, Kent, but you made it yours when you took it into your own mind and gave it form in your own words. That's writing, Kent, and writing goes quite a way beyond a school composition."

Kent looked at her, not entirely sure what she was saying except that she was telling him she was pleased with his composition.

"What did you say was the name of the man with whom you have talked?"

"I didn't say, but it's Mr. John Rivven. I think he is some kind of an artist."

"There is a John Rivven who is a very well known artist and I understand that he has recently come to live in these parts, but"—she paused, then shook her head—"he must be a very busy man."

"This Mr. Rivven is never too busy. He always has time for a talk."

"Perhaps it's another person altogether."

"This Mr. Rivven has a hive of bees."

"Well, then, that explains it; if he's just a beekeeper he might well have time to discuss local history and such. Quite possibly you're mistaken about the name, Kent."

"But, Miss Hinshaw," Kent began, eager to say something about the drawings he had twice seen, then he shut his lips tightly. What did it matter the name his friend went by? He didn't carry a county the way Kent did in his.

Tossing his book satchel over his shoulders, Kent soon left the schoolroom. Only Tessa remained outside, waiting for him.

"You always walk home by way of the Downs, don't you?" she asked.

"Yes."

"May I walk along with you?"

In answer, Kent took her satchel from her and slung it over his shoulder.

"I didn't know you could write," Tessa said.

"Write? What do you mean?"

"Your composition that Miss Hinshaw read."

"She can call it writing if she wants to, but it's really just talking—putting down on paper the things I say inside myself."

"I liked it."

"I liked yours, too. Everyone did."

They walked along in silence for a while.

"Isn't it much farther for you to walk home by the Downs than through the churchyard the way most of the children do?"

Kent kicked a stone before him in the road. "I've got my own reasons."

"So you know Uncle John!" Tessa exclaimed.

"Who?"

"Mr. John Rivven, the artist."

"I expect that I don't know him as well as you do," Kent admitted.

Tessa beamed with her knowledge. "My mum helps out for him now and then, and when she goes over to Beekeep I go with her.

He has a housekeeper, Mrs. Talbot from Petham, but she's old and she has her own house to care for and she can't do everything for him."

They were walking more slowly now for suddenly there seemed so much to talk about. Each one had been enriched by friendship with a stranger newly come to Chilham and each was ready to share the riches with the other.

In the distance before them Kent saw the outlines of Beekeep, snuggling into a fold of the hills, its tile roof neatly overhanging plaster and timbered walls. No sign of life was about it. No curl of smoke came from its chimney. Whatever life it contained it was keeping to itself that day. Perhaps the artist was at home, putting

finishing touches on the canvases he had started outdoors. Perhaps he was away. It was a dull day in any case and the wind that whipped around Tessa and Kent had the raw edge of coming winter to it.

"Uncle John's in London today," Tessa announced as they passed the cottage. "He had to take some of his pictures to an exhibition."

Beyond Beekeep, by a quarter of a mile, was another cottage. The nearer they got to it the more aware Kent became of the life that throbbed within it. Smoke rose invitingly from its chimney. An early light shone behind one of its many-paned windows. A large washing, with clothes that would fit a wide variety of sizes, hung limp from a long line. The November wind might have done plenty of airing but it had accomplished little drying. Cheerful sounds came from within the cottage, and the smell of baking was on the air.

"Here's home," Tessa said with a smile and a quickening of her steps.

Kent went as far as the small gate in the gorse hedge that surrounded the cottage, then he stopped.

"Come along, won't you? Mum's always glad to have one more."

Kent shook his head. Seeing Tessa's home teeming with living had sent a surge of feeling through him that made him acutely conscious of the difference between her life and his. Feeling lonely, he wanted to be alone. "My mum is home from work today. I should be there to help her."

To be needed in the household was something that Tessa clearly understood. She smiled agreement and started through the gate. "Your mum will be glad to know about the high mark you got in composition."

"She'll be surprised."

"So will my mum."

Kent handed Tessa her satchel and they said good-by. Tessa ran the short distance to the cottage door and disappeared inside. Kent started back over the path that went along the Downs and into Chilham. After he had passed Beekeep, there was no other cottage for nearly a mile.

Once he was on the open path with the wind buffeting him, Kent felt more like himself. He put his hands in his pockets to warm them and found some granules of earth to finger. It was as if the earth had something wonderful to it. Rolling it between his fingers made him mindful of all the others before him whose earth it had been. The sharp sense of aloneness began to ease away and he felt himself in the company of those people who had shared the land before he had come to call it his.

In the satchel bumping against his back that held books and the necessities of his school day was the composition. He was not quite sure what his mother would say when she read it, but he was almost certain that Mr. Rivven would say, "It isn't finished yet, is it? I expect there's more you'd like to do to it." And there was, Kent told himself, a great deal more.

The idea within the composition was like one of the mulberry cuttings. It had its own growing to do. It would be a long time before it could gain the stature of a tree and then perform the functions of a tree, producing in its time and with the seasons bud, blossom, and fruit. It would be a far longer time before he could say in words what he felt inside himself. Kent had so much thinking to do that it seemed only a few minutes before he had neared the village and was starting down the slope on the road that led to the Lees. Then it was his own home that was before him and he was opening the door and calling to his mother.

The room that served most of their living was warm and cozy, for Maidey had been doing a large wash and was now on the last of her ironing. She had scrubbed the floor, swept the carpet, wiped the windows, and polished the copper kettle until it shone with the red tongue of flame from the coal beneath it. Her one free day of the week was something she lived for and then lived in. On it she could do to her own house what she did on five days of the week to another's.

Looking up from her ironing as Kent came in, she greeted him with her all-too-rare smile. Her face was flushed. Her hair, usually drawn back smooth and severe, had been escaping around her face and she lifted a hand to push it away. She rested her iron for a moment to talk with her son.

"It's beautiful, Mum," Kent said, as he gazed around the room admiringly. He had said that every Thursday afternoon for almost as long as he could remember.

Maidey accepted the compliment. "I like to keep things nice for you, Kent."

Kent wrinkled his nose.

She laughed. "You're right. It's a bit of roasting pork that I've got in the oven, and there'll be an apple dumpling to follow."

"I'm hungry, Mum; I don't know as I can wait much longer."

"Have a biscuit then, for there'll be no supper until I finish this ironing and until you go up to the Square for me."

Kent ate a biscuit slowly while his mother gave him a short list of errands to do for her. She had received her weekly wages the previous day and with them she could pay the amounts owing various tradesmen. "And when you come back, Kent, fill the coal box and put another chunk on the fire, then wash yourself good and clean. The roast will be ready by that time." She handed him three separate envelopes, each containing its exact amount of money. Impulsively she put her arm around him and kissed him, smoothing her hand over his hair.

Kent left the house and retraced his steps to the Square. He wanted to get the errands done as quickly as possible so he could return to the smell of pork and the warm comfort of his own home. Thursday, he thought to himself, was something like Christmas; perhaps it was even better, for Christmas happened only once a year and there was a Thursday in every week.

It was not until after the roast pork and the apple dumplings had been eaten, the dishes washed and put away, that Kent opened his satchel and handed the composition to his mother. She made a rippling sound of pleasure when she saw the high mark in the left-hand corner and read under it the few words of commendation Miss Hinshaw had written.

"Read it, Mum, read it for yourself."

Maidey took the two pages and spread them flat on the table, then she moved the lamp nearer her. Kent folded his arms on the table and sunk his head in them, keeping his eyes on his mother. Once before that day he had been in torment when his words had been read, but that had been a torment of embarrassment; now it was one of fear lest his mother should not like what he had written.

He did not know what he would do if she did not like it. It was almost more than he could bear to watch her as she read, but he could not bear to take his eyes off her for even a moment.

Maidey read slowly, forming the words silently with her lips. Every now and then she moistened her lips with her tongue as if the silent effort dried them. Sometimes she went back and reread a whole sentence as if she had not got the gist of it at first. She turned the first page over after she had read it and set it aside on the table, then she devoted herself to the second page. As she neared the end, she began to move her head slowly up and down. "I never knew there was so much to a mulberry tree," she said. In her voice was admiration tinged with wonder that it was her own son who was telling her these things.

Kent lifted his head hopefully.

"However did you come to know all this—" she started to ask, then paused. Her glance was still on the paper as she brought the two pages together. A quivering of the muscles across her forehead told of perplexity. When she looked up and across the table at Kent, it was with troubled eyes. "Or did you make it up?"

If there was one thing in life that Maidey Conner wanted for her son it was for him to be honest. To speak the truth and to have good manners was essential; all else was incidental. The high mark would have been worthless if, in achieving it, Kent had dealt in falsehood.

Kent met her gaze without wavering. "I didn't make it up, Mum. I said what Mr. Rivven told me, only I said it in my own way."

"Are you sure it is all right to do that?"

"Yes, Mum. Miss Hinshaw says it is. And besides, whenever Mr. Rivven tells me anything, he always asks me what I think and I have to put it in my own words to know what I think."

The frown slid away from Maidey's brow and relief relaxed her face.

"Miss Hinshaw says when you make something your own and say it in your own words that you're really writing, and writing is more than doing a composition."

"Writing," Maidey echoed the word, then she looked at Kent curiously. She said nothing for a moment. "Writing," she repeated.

"I'd like for you not to go getting any notions, Kent, at least not yet."

"Notions?"

"You're to learn a trade when you finish school, and that's how you're to make your way in the world."

"Yes, Mum." Kent wondered why it had become necessary to assure his mother of something he had always known he would do. "I'll make a good living for both of us as soon as I start to work, I promise you, Mum."

"All I ask is that you learn to do a good day's work." Maidey paused to listen to the distant striking of the hour from the clock in the tower of St. Mary's. "Bedtime," she announced.

For a long time after Kent had gone upstairs to the small room under the eaves, Maidey sat at the table with the lamp turned low. The fire in the grate had been diminishing in warmth and she had thrown a shawl over her shoulders against the creeping cold of the night. She read the composition through once again. Moved, as she had not been at the earlier reading, by the last line *"It is the growing that matters,"* she said it over and over to herself as she stared at the words. For years her one aim had been to do the best thing for Kent and she had been quite sure that she knew what that was. Now a seed of doubt had got caught in her mind. No longer did she feel that she could rightly say what his growing might be.

Pilgrims' Way

4

November moved on into December with shorter hours of daylight and less sunshine. If the sun appeared in the morning, it rarely lasted until the time of its setting, and warmth seemed to have utterly gone from it. The wind blew in from the east with rain in its wake; when it shifted to the west the clearing was often of short duration. Fields were sodden and lanes muddy, but the path Kent took along the Downs on his way home from school was generally firm.

From one part of it he could see the reedy twistings of the river Stour and follow with his eyes for more than a mile the way the waterfowl traveled. Marshland merged into meadows and meadows into fallow fields, but all was quiet and empty as winter's cold lay over the land. Farther along the path he could look ahead and see the whole village of Chilham, on a hill and cradled by hills.

If he climbed up to the turrets of the castle, he could see across the tile roofs of the brick and timber-framed village houses all the way to the square tower of St. Mary's. Everything was neat and tidy, self-respecting his mother called it, but there was little sign of life. In the damp and the chill and the early coming dark, most of the people found that their activity lay within doors.

He could not see the Woolpack Inn at the bottom of the hill, but he knew it was there, as much the center of the village as it had been in the days when smugglers made it their rendezvous, often escaping by the underground passage that led from the inn up to the castle.

The view of St. Mary's was clear, now that the lime trees surrounding the ancient church were bare of leaves. The chequered flint-and-stone tower merged into the leaden sky behind it. The flag that fluttered from the tower was filled with wind from the west, sure sign that there would be no more rain. There was even a shaft of light breaking through the rapidly moving clouds.

"A fine day, indeed, or what's left of it!" Kent exclaimed. He breathed deeply, as if he were breathing into himself the rounded hills behind him and the neat little village before him.

He turned for a moment to watch the light in the west spread across the sky, spilling such a golden haze over the countryside that everything was tinged with beauty. A barely perceptible line of mist was rising along the river. In the intensity of light it looked as if the river's breath was gold.

The countryside might be empty of the sight of any people, but the air carried the sound of someone at work. For a considerable distance, Kent had been hearing the ring of an ax upon wood. The sound became clearer and more resonant as he drew nearer its source, then he saw before him a man who was cutting branches from a limb that had fallen across the path. Even the back view of the man was familiar. Kent broke into a run to cover the remaining distance between them.

John Rivven stopped cutting and leaned on his ax. "You're just in time to lend me a hand," he said, as if he had been waiting for Kent to appear.

"How did you know I'd be coming this way?"

"Tessa told me you always walked the long way, for one thing. And for another, the day is as fine as any we can get in mid-December."

Kent looked pleased. He was trying to recall something his mother had told him to do, but before he could remember what it was, John Rivven was pointing to the limb on the ground.

"I haven't got another tool, but if you'll drag away what I've cut we'll soon have this job done. Big, isn't it? It must have come down in last night's wind."

Kent dragged away one of the branches, placing it parallel to the path as Mr. Rivven had already done with some others. "Not many people use this path now, at least not this time of year."

"True," John Rivven agreed, "but a path is something to be kept open, any roadway is, and this one traverses half of southern England. From Southwark to Canterbury is still something of a journey; it must have been considerably more of one when feet and hoofs made it." He glanced at Kent. "Things going a bit better?"

Kent nodded. "I've had good marks for a fortnight."

"Tessa told me of your composition. I think she remembered every word."

"Did you mind my writing about what you had told me?"

"Did you mind my putting you in the picture with the heron?"

"Of course not! It was your picture."

"Just so, it was your composition. You did with it what you wanted to do. I might almost say what you had to do. That's art."

"My mother says that artists—" Kent stopped. Now he remembered what it was his mother had told him to do. She had told him to be sure and say thank you twice over for the times he had accepted Mr. Rivven's hospitality. Kent hastened to say the words before anything else could happen that might make him forget.

Even as he spoke, he knew that to satisfy his mother he should have addressed Mr. Rivven as "sir." It was what he would have done in any other case with the sort of gentleman Mr. Rivven obviously was, but Kent had not been able to use the title even at their first meeting. He could not have explained why, to his mother or to anyone else. "Sir" was not a form of address used for either a friend or a relative, and this stranger whom Kent met on occasions had become to him something of a friendly relative.

Kent felt respectful with John Rivven, as he did with any older person, but he could not muster formality. To have given him a title would have been as out of place as a January wind blowing through a June garden, yet Kent knew that his mother would have been bitterly disappointed if she had known that Kent did not address Mr. Rivven properly.

John Rivven nodded solemnly. "Thanks are duly accepted, and with them I am reminded that it must be nearly time for tea. We're not far from Beekeep and tea will be ready for us there today. Do you suppose we can make a hitch with rope and drag this piece of limb down with us? It has burning enough in it to be a yule log." He took some rope from his pocket and handed one end to Kent.

Kent walked around the length of oak, no longer a limb but a roughly hewn log. It was sound enough, save on one side where rot had set in. The gale, catching it in its weakened place, had torn it from the tree trunk. Kent looked up into the branches overhead. The oak was huge. It could stand the loss of a limb, even as mighty a one as lay sprawled across the path. "It must be a very ancient tree!"

"Oh indeed," John Rivven said, "a thousand years, at least." He started to lash his piece of rope around one end of the log while Kent secured his piece at the other end. Between them, enough slack was left for hauling.

As John Rivven worked he talked, and Kent listened as he helped. "It would have been a young tree when the pilgrims came along on their way to St. Thomas's shrine at Canterbury, telling their stories. And long before even the oak grew here the path was being traveled. Perhaps an earlier oak shed an acorn that became this tree, or perhaps the seed fell from a passing person's pouch. Those were the days when the Phoenicians anchored their ships on the Kentish coast and tramped over this path to the tin mines in Cornwall, then back again with their load of the precious metal."

"Why didn't they sail around to the Cornish coast; wouldn't it have been easier?"

"The history books may give you a reason or two, but who is ever to know why a man will pursue one way rather than another?"

Kent looked up from the knot he was tying to smile his quick flashing smile. He knew as well as the dark-skinned Phoenicians that he had his own reasons for walking on the ancient path. In a moment of time, he felt sudden kinship with people who had stood two thousand years ago where he was standing now.

John Rivven tested the knots and took some of the slack in his hands, then he placed the rest of the slack in Kent's hands. "It's going to take some real pulling power. Don't you think we'd do a better job if we felt we were related?"

The play of a word had made Kent feel a closeness with the ancient Phoenicians; now the urgency of need made him feel equally close to one Mr. Rivven. "You mean if I call you Uncle John the way Tessa does?"

"Exactly. I think, Kent, we'll put our hearts into our work as well as our muscles. Now, pull hard when I say *ho*. Are you quite ready?"

"Yes, Uncle John," Kent said as he grasped his end of the rope tightly and set his stance.

"Heave—*ho!*"

They pulled and the log moved, slowly at first, unwillingly; then, as their effort became more coordinated, the log moved steadily.

"It's downhill to Beekeep—and not very far—and mostly straight," John Rivven said, his words setting a rhythm that matched their tugging. "On the last bit—we may have to hold back—instead of pull—so the log won't get away from us—on the slope. Heave—*ho,* heave we go!"

When they reached the cottage, they rolled the log against a wall where it would have the benefit of the sun for drying. An old straw-tiered beehive stood nearby. John Rivven laid his hand on the hive, then kneeling, he bent his face close to it.

"The bees are taking their winter sleep," he explained, "but, even so, I like to tell them when someone is coming to the cottage who has never been here before and who may often come again."

"It's nice to feel related to you," Kent said as he followed the artist up the path to his cottage door. "Of course, I have my mother, but I haven't had a father for a long time. My own is dead."

There was such a sense of sadness in the boy's words that the man turned back toward him and laid his hand on his shoulder. "We don't ever lose what we can remember, Kent," he said gently.

Kent lifted his face. His eyes were dark with a passion he felt safe to express. "That's the trouble, Uncle John, I can't remember him. Even when I try, there's nothing there."

John Rivven nodded as if he understood, then he led the way through the nail-studded door into a room that seemed to Kent to consist only of a large open fireplace and walls lined with books.

A small fire was burning in the deep, wide hearth near which was a comfortable chair and a table with many books. On another table was a tea tray. John Rivven switched on a lamp and moved a chair near to the fire for Kent. Kent could see now that there was more to the room than the huge fireplace, but that was its heart.

"We've come just in time," John Rivven said as he lifted the big blue tea cozy that stood on the tray. Under it was a teapot with steam wavering from its spout. He took the cover from a dish to reveal a pile of buttered crumpets. "Sit down, Kent." The artist sat down in his own chair and started to pour tea into one of the cups. "Let's see, how is it you take your tea—milk and plenty of sugar?"

Kent nodded. He didn't care how he got his tea. He was sure that he must be dreaming. No, not quite sure. There were blisters from the rope on his hands and they spoke for something, but what it was he could scarcely recall. After he had consumed one of the crumpets and swallowed half of the tea in his cup, his sense of reality returned. "How did this all happen, Uncle John?"

"Tea? Well, it's time for it, and my housekeeper had good warning that there would be two of us when she saw us bumping the log along the path."

"It's wonderful." Kent helped himself to another crumpet when it was offered to him.

"It's always people who make wonderful things happen."

Kent waited expectantly for his friend's often-voiced coda "Or is it?" but it did not come. This was not something then for discussion or even individual pursuit. This was a statement of fact. Kent held it before his mind as he might a curious stone before his eyes and studied it. He found he agreed with the statement. Wonderful things did not just happen. It was people who brought them about, people who somehow cared.

They might have talked about a multitude of things in that twilight tea-time hour, but each one seemed content to savor in silence the comfort that surrounded him, as well as the assurance of the other's company. The room grew dusky. Kent knew that he should soon be leaving, but he could not bear to remove himself from the circle of warmth by the fire and the many books, everyone of which he wished he might someday read.

A door opened at one end of the room, letting in a stream of light and the good smell of the dinner that was cooking. A comfortable, gray-haired woman wearing a neat white apron came in.

John Rivven stirred in his chair. "Mrs. Talbot, I'd like you to meet my new nephew, Kent Conner."

Kent stood up and held out his hand to the housekeeper.

"Another one?" She looked at Kent appraisingly, then shook his hand. "You're welcome to Beekeep."

After she had gone back to the kitchen with the tea tray, Kent remained standing, knowing that it was time to go and knowing that if he sat down again he would never want to go. He spoke his thanks and started toward the door.

"The next fine day may well be Christmas," John Rivven said.

"It often rains at Christmas."

"And so it may, but Christmas makes its own weather. It's the one day of the year that is always fine."

Kent could nod in agreement. "It is, at that, Uncle John. My mother never has to go to work on Christmas Day, nor on Boxing Day either."

Opening the door, John Rivven exclaimed, "I say, but it has got dark while we've been having our tea! Wouldn't you like a flash-light?"

"It isn't all that dark, Uncle John, and I know the way, but thank you, thank you very much indeed."

John Rivven stood in the open doorway and watched Kent travel along the beam of light that reached out from the house. When he could no longer see the boy, he closed the door and went back to stand by the fire. Mrs. Talbot came in to draw the curtains and put a new log on the fire.

"He's a nicely mannered boy," she commented.

"I'm glad you think well of him. He's lonely and a bit afraid of life, but he has something to him. I think he may go far if he's given half a chance."

"That's what you say about them all. If this lad is who I think he is, he won't easily get even that amount of a chance. His mother does housework in Canterbury. I don't know anything against her. She's honest and self-respecting, and I can see that she's bringing her boy up well, but she has nothing."

"Nothing?"

"That's what they say in the village. Now, Mr. Rivven, please tell me if you've made any arrangements for your Christmas dinner. I'll come to cook it and do for you on that day if you've no one else, but I'd like to be with my own daughter and her children if you don't need me."

John Rivven was silent. He nodded his head slowly as if he were doing his best to consider Mrs. Talbot's wishes, then he turned to face the fire and poke at it with his foot. When he finally turned back to face the woman who was waiting for her answer, he spoke firmly. "Mrs. Talbot, you are to have Christmas Day for yourself, and not only the day but the week as well."

An unbelieving smile softened the lines of the housekeeper's face. "Has the gypsy-girl's mother offered to do for you then?"

"No, Tessa's mother has her hands too full with her household of children. It's someone, well"—he paused and looked at her as if to beg indulgence for some matter he preferred to keep to himself for a while—"it's someone extremely capable, but I'd rather not say anything about it just yet."

Mrs. Talbot moved her head in perfect understanding. "Now, I am glad to hear that, Mr. Rivven. If I may say so, you've come to your senses at last. I've always told you there were plenty of good women walking the earth."

John Rivven stared at her, then he started to laugh outright. "But, Mrs. Talbot, I—"

"That's all right, Mr. Rivven, I can keep another's affairs as I do my own to myself, but as you know I can't keep house for you always. I'm getting on in years and I'd like to be able to help my daughter before I get too old to help anyone. It's not that you're hard to please, Mr. Rivven. All you need is someone to take care of you." Mrs. Talbot went toward the kitchen. At the door she turned back and said, "You know as well as I do that the Bible says it's not good for a man to live alone."

John Rivven sat down in his chair. He felt helpless, first with laughter at the situation that had apparently been established, and then at the realization that no matter what their discussion Mrs. Talbot always came out on top. Ever since she had kept house for him she had ruled him with an unquestioned hand. When she became convinced, there was never any dissuading her. Well, he sighed inwardly as well as outwardly, he had given her Christmas Day and the week to follow and that had made her happy. When she returned from her long-deserved holiday he would straighten her out in her misconception.

He knew quite well, he reminded himself, that she would never leave him for that holiday unless he could give her solemn assurance that someone was coming in to cook his dinner. There was no harm in asking Mrs. Conner if she would do just that. If she brought Kent with her and if Tessa was asked to help, it might make a reasonably cheerful thing out of what could be a rather lonely day. Mrs. Talbot need never know until she returned how wrong she had been. He would write a note and give it to Tessa to give to Kent in school tomorrow, and Kent could deliver it to his mother.

The letter, duly written, changed hands three times before Maidey opened it and read the words that asked her to cook dinner on Christmas Day at Beekeep Cottage. She was to bring Kent along and Tessa would be there to help with the washing up.

Maidey read the letter through twice before she looked up to face Kent, who had not taken his eyes off her all the time she was reading. "There won't be much washing up if there's just the four to dinner."

"Mum, will you do it?"

"Well, the day is mine to do as I like with it, but I've never worked for money on Christmas Day."

"Mum, *will* you do it? Oh, Mum, please say yes!"

Maidey folded the letter and put it back in its envelope while Kent waited in an agony of suspense as to what her word would be.

"I suppose one job is no different from another and we all have to eat."

"Then you will do it, Mum?"

Maidey was not yet ready to say yes. "I wish he were anything but an artist."

"Why, Mum?"

"Artists are"—she paused, reaching for words that would somehow express to Kent what she felt about artists—"they are untidy people."

"Mum, his house is very neat and clean, and he's a nice-appearing gentleman."

"He has a housekeeper to do for him. Besides, I don't mean his house, Kent."

Kent knew when he should say no more. He sat down at the table and opened one of his schoolbooks. At least he could pretend to read even if his mind had taken him ahead into the next week.

"I'll have to find out whether it's a roast of beef he'll be wanting, or a goose. Most likely it will be a goose; they're prime at this season." Maidey went on talking to herself as she thought out loud. "If it is a goose, then I'll have to find out what stuffing he prefers. Chestnut or apple. He might want both. If he does, I'll put the chestnut in the crop and the apple in the body cavity. There'll be mashed potatoes and boiled onions and—"

Kent looked up from his book and stared at his mother as she planned the kitchen dinner from the main course to the flaming plum pudding, then the tangerines and the nuts.

"And coffee, of course. He'll take his strong and black, most likely, but there'll be some with a dash of milk in it for you children."

She had given her answer.

"Mum, we've never had a dinner like that!"

Her eyes were shining as she returned from her world of kitchen wonder to face Kent. "Yes we have, Kent, and more than once, but you were too young to remember."

"When will you let them know at Beekeep?"

"I'll give you a letter for Mr. Rivven when you go off to school tomorrow. If you leave it at his house on your way home in the afternoon, he'll know soon enough. There is still more than a week to Christmas."

The Long Arm of the Past

5

Another exchange of notes between Maidey Conner and John Rivven settled the question of the menu for the Christmas dinner. A goose it was to be, with all that went with it. Tessa's mother would stuff it and make it ready for the oven, and Tessa would see that it went into the oven at the proper hour. If, John Rivven said in his note, Maidey arrived by eleven o'clock on Christmas morning, she would have ample time to prepare the rest of the dinner, baste the bird as the roasting progressed, and have all in order for the four of them to sit down at half past one.

Maidey felt as if her work had been cut unreasonably short. She would have preferred to have had every detail in her own hands and she could well have done so by reaching Beekeep at an earlier hour. Mr. Rivven made no explanation of the time schedule which he had so carefully set up, but Maidey knew there were considerations that had to be taken into account. She read the letter through methodically, then slipped it into the pocket of her dress for occasional reference. She knew her orders when she received them.

"It doesn't seem as if I was to have much to do," Maidey commented to Kent, "with Tessa's mum preparing the bird and Tessa putting it into the oven."

"When are we to get to Beekeep?"

"At eleven o'clock on the morning of Christmas Day," Maidey said with precision. "Mr. Rivven had his reasons for not wanting us to arrive any sooner."

Kent glanced at the clock that ticked away on the wall, but it was a calendar he needed. There was still almost a week of days to pass.

Every morning, when Kent started off to school, Maidey gave him a message to deliver to Tessa. "Tell her she must be sure to keep the heat of the oven even and not too hot. A bird does better when it is gentled." "Tell her to baste the bird every fifteen minutes until I get there, and not only with the drippings but with a squeeze of orange juice to cut the grease." "Tell her—"

"Don't you have any messages for Uncle John?" Kent asked one morning near the end of the school week.

Maidey glanced up at him quickly. "So that's what you've come to with him, is it?"

"That's what Tessa calls him, Mum. It's natural-like for me to call him that, too."

Maidey was silent for a moment. "Well," she finally admitted, "I suppose there's no harm in it. You've no one of your own to call by such a name."

"Mum, do you have any messages for him?"

She shook her head. "I told him that I'd look after the dinner and that we'd be there at the time he set. There's nothing more to be said."

Maidey's free Thursday before Christmas was an unusually busy day for her. There was her house to be cleaned and her washing to be done, and there was extra work as well. Her black dress had to be pressed, and the coat she wore only on Sunday mornings when she went to church had to be both sponged and pressed. It had seen more years than Kent had but it was a good coat, purchased at Harrod's when she had once spent a week in London. Of recent years it had had more care than wear.

"Once a good coat always a good coat," she assured herself as she brushed it prior to sponging it. The saying would not hold for

Kent's clothes. A growing boy was hard on everything he wore. Maidey did what she could to keep jackets and trousers going as long as it was decently possible, but they seemed to be always wearing out. If I could just get him something really good for once, it might last him longer than these cheap things, she thought. But an expensive suit of clothes was not practical while he was growing, or possible in any case.

Kent, when he came home from school that Thursday afternoon, took off his wool jacket and trousers and pulled on an old sweater and a pair of corduroy pants. Maidey, holding the jacket up to the light, studied it for thin places that might require some reinforcement. She did the same with the trousers, then she tested the buttons.

"Whatever it is you've got in that right-hand pocket I'll be pleased to have you remove before I do any sponging and pressing."

Kent took the trousers from her. Standing by the table, he emptied the contents of the pocket onto the surface that Maidey had polished an hour before. As much as a teaspoonful of earth trickled out onto the bare table.

Maidey gasped. "Kent! My clean table—all that dirt! What are you doing?" She reached hastily for a cloth and would have swept the disturbing grains away had not Kent laid his hand on her arm.

"It's not dirt, Mum. It's England."

Maidey dropped the cloth and stared at him. "Whatever do you mean? It's dirt, plain dirt, the kind you bring in on your boots, the kind that people track into their houses and that I spend my life sweeping away."

"Perhaps," Kent said, "but it's earth the little ancient people loved enough to fight for and the Romans took. It's earth the pilgrims trod on their way to Canterbury and that I walk over to school. It was theirs once, and now it is ours, and it's England, Mum. Don't you recognize it?" He smiled at her, then with his fingers guided the earth into a neat little pile.

Kent's words did nothing to Maidey. She was scarcely aware of them, impassioned as they were, but his smile was tantalizing. It teased something in her mind, something that had been forgotten for so long that it had all but gone into oblivion. She reached across the table with her hand, letting her finger tips touch the tiny pile that lay between them.

"English earth," she murmured. She sat down heavily and leaned against the table.

"Take some, Mum." Kent smiled again at her hesitation, at her finger tips caressing the earth as if she did not quite dare to handle it.

"Take of English earth as much
As either hand may rightly clutch—"

Kent, as he said the words, felt them to be as vivid and strong in his mind as a banner waving in the breeze.

"Oh, Kent!" Maidey drew in her breath quickly, then she stroked the earth with a finger cautiously. "Can you say the rest of it?"

"The rest of it? You mean the words belong to something, and that there are more?"

"Yes, oh, yes, Kent, many more words."

She smiled now as she looked into Kent's face. She picked up some of the grains from the little pile and let them slide slowly through her fingers.

Kent, who had found the words in his mind with no idea of their origin or extent, was overcome by longing to know the rest that belonged to the few he had discovered. "Say it, Mum, say it all from the beginning to the end. I want to know."

Maidey paused; her lips moved but not with words.

"Mum, I've *got* to know."

"Wait, Kent. It's so far away, so long ago, it's something I haven't thought of for years and years."

"Mum, please—" Kent waited for the thin strand to appear that would link him to something he, too, had forgotten, if he had ever known it.

Maidey put her hands across her eyes as if, in shutting out the present scene, she could the better find her way into the past. "I think," she began, "it goes like this—" In a low, singsong tone that was different from her usual voice she began to speak. Kent, listening, held his breath as if the slightest sound might break his mother's train of thought.

"In the taking of it breathe
Prayer for all who lie beneath—
Not the great nor well bespoke,
But the mere uncounted folk
Of whose death is none
Report or lamentation."

She hesitated, but did not remove her hands from her eyes.

Kent, breathing lightly, waited for her to come to the end that she was trying to reach.

"Lay that earth upon thy heart,
And thy sickness shall depart!"

There was silence in the room. The ticking of the clock, the whisper of coal burning in the grate, the brush of wind outside against the glass, only served to deepen the silence. Perhaps there is still more, Kent thought, and for it he would have waited indefinitely. He kept his eyes on his mother, who had somehow become someone he had never known before, someone who could bring from an inner depth words that stirred and comforted him, the way Uncle John was able to do.

Maidey laid her hands on the table and looked at Kent brightly. She smiled as if she was undeniably pleased with something she had done. "There now, I've said it, the first verse in any case." Her voice became matter-of-fact again when she said, "I never would have thought I could have remembered it. It's been years since I've heard it said, but I used to hear it often."

"What is it, Mum? It sounds like a song."

"And so it is, I suppose, a kind of song. Your father used to read it to you from a book that was filled with suchlike poems, and there were stories in it, too. But, Kent, you were such a little boy, only three or so; how is it you came to remember the first lines? Without them I would never have thought of the rest."

"It wasn't remembering. They were there in my mind like"—Kent paused to think of a way he could explain to his mother what it was like—"the way snowdrops are in the ground, or bluebells. They just appear when the weather is right."

"Your father used to read a lot to you, Kent, even when you were a baby, and you always listened as if you understood the words."

"Did he often read the poem that you've just said to me?"

"Oh, yes." Maidey smiled with remembering. "And there were many more verses to it. He read it often and often. He was especially fond of it. That was why—" She stopped short. The smile fled from her face.

"Why what?"

"Why the words that are on his stone in the graveyard are as they are. You've seen them."

"I never go through the new graveyard."

"Well, perhaps that's as it should be. It's no place for a growing boy."

Or is it? Kent caught the words with his tongue against his lips before they came out. They were not so important just then as the book that held the poem. Wondering where it might be, he glanced around the small room that enclosed most of their living. Perhaps it was in a drawer of the dresser. Perhaps it was in the box with his mother's best tablecloth. Hungry for the book, Kent felt acutely aware of the cold bare walls of their cottage, of the plaster that showed in places where the damp came through. He thought longingly of the book-lined walls in Uncle John's sitting room.

"Where is that book, Mum?"

Maidey did not seem to hear the question so Kent repeated it.

"It was sold, Kent, some years ago, with all your father's things. I had my reasons."

"Didn't you keep anything?"

Maidey felt the reproach in her son's voice and was silent before it.

Kent thought of the boxes under the eaves of the little room where he slept. He knew they contained a change of clothing that was brought out in the warm weather and his mother's best tea set which was never brought out. He felt sure that there must be other things in those boxes. He didn't care how little there was as long as there was something.

"Yes, I kept a few things, Kent. There was no need to keep many." She sighed. "I wouldn't expect you to understand, Kent; you're too young, but when you lose most that's real in life it's better to let the rest go, too."

"But Mum, Mum, you can't lose what you can remember."

"Whoever said that to you?"

"It's true, isn't it?"

She nodded. Her lips were drawn tight. "There are some things I don't want to remember."

"But I do," Kent said, "and between us"—he smiled at the sudden thought—"Mum, between us we remembered the poem that I never knew and that you thought you'd forgot."

"We did at that, and it did us no harm. Kent, you've not talked with Mr. Rivven about your father, have you?"

"No, Mum, not really." Surprise was large on the boy's face. "Just to say—"

Maidey got up from the table and went to a drawer in the dresser from which she took a small box. Opening the box, she removed something from it and returned to the table. Near the little pile of earth she laid a silver nutmeg that was black with tarnish. "Here's something your father gave me once. You can't read what's written on it, it's so black; but it says *Souvenir of Ramsgate*."

Kent stared at the trinket that had taken its place beside the pile of earth on the table.

"I remember that I asked him what it was good for and he said, in that offhanded way of his, that if I kept it for seven years I might find a use for it." Maidey moved a finger across the fingers of her other hand, counting all five and back two. "It's an odd thing, but it's just gone seven years."

Kent, handling the nutmeg, discovered that it opened. "Look, Mum, it's big enough to hold this bit of earth!" He reached for a spoon and began to fill the nutmeg. When it was full he closed the two halves and rubbed it against his sleeve to remove some of the tarnish.

"And that's that," Maidey said as she might when reading a book at the close of a chapter.

"Yes, that's that!" Kent repeated, eager to find in the book just opening someone he had never had a chance to know.

Lengthening Yule

6

On Christmas morning Kent and his mother walked along the path that would take them to Beekeep. Kent's arms swung free; Maidey carried a brown paper bag in which was her apron. They were silent, as they generally were when walking together. Maidey was going over in her mind for the hundredth time the various stages of the dinner she would soon be preparing. Kent had a sense of expectancy about the day that made it different from any Christmas he had ever known before, or any day for that matter.

"It's fine, Mum, isn't it?" he said, breathing the damp air that came rolling up from the river to meet the thin December sunshine.

"It's seasonable."

Over their breakfast teacups they had exchanged presents with each other. Maidey's for Kent had been a pair of warm woolen socks, wrapped in a piece of brown paper and tied with a strand of the wool. She had made the socks in her free time, most of which was on the bus going to and from her work in Canterbury, and she had kept them carefully hidden from Kent so he would not know what she was doing for him. Kent was delighted with them and lost no time in taking off the ones he was wearing and putting on the new ones.

"They fit me well, Mum, and they're warm."

"They'll do." Maidey was pleased that the fit was good. "Socks made by hand have more wear to them than the machined kind," she said.

Kent had given her a small box, so carefully wrapped that Maidey had a time undoing it, and while she was still opening it he had to tell her in his excitement what it was. "It's a silver chain, Mum, for your silver nutmeg!"

Maidey uncoiled the chain and held it up, looking at the play of light on the broad flat links, then with a gay gesture she put it around her neck. She got up and went to the dresser drawer for the nutmeg. When she removed it from its box she exclaimed happily, for Kent had cleaned and polished it so that it shone as it had when it was new. Maidey rolled it about in her palm.

"Now, you can read what it says, Kent—*Souvenir of Ramsgate*. I'll clip it to the chain and then I can wear it like a piece of jewelry."

"The chain isn't really silver, Mum."

"I expect the nutmeg is only plate, but the two of them do look nice together."

"I got it, Mum, at the shop in the Square. It's really a dog chain, but Mr. Peters cut it short so it would be the right length for a necklace. He only charged me half price because he kept the rest, and he put the catch on free. I'd been doing errands for him all afternoon and it was my pay, so to speak."

"Oh, Kent," Maidey said, as she held the chain and the nutmeg in her hands, "you couldn't have given me anything I would care for more."

"Will you wear it, Mum, today?"

She would not look at Kent, for at that moment she was not sure which Kent she might see. Time had slipped for her and she was living again in the hour when the silver nutmeg had first been given to her. Holding it in her palm, she had admired it and wondered at it, then she had looked up into her husband's eyes wanting to say her thanks for something he had given her whose only apparent use was her adornment. All she had been able to say was to ask him what it was for.

He had laughed at her consternation and told her she would find a use for it, even if she had to wait seven years. Closing her hands over the nutmeg and the chain, she looked up at Kent, who had been watching her closely, waiting for her decision. She nodded.

"Then let me have it, Mum, please, and I'll clip the nutmeg to the chain."

While Kent worked to secure the two together, Maidey went to the stove to get the rashers of bacon that were their Christmas treat. When she returned to the table, Kent fastened the chain around her neck.

"Now you're dressed up for a party," he said, "just as I am in my new socks."

So they had had their presents and there were no more to be opened, yet Kent felt as they walked along the path that the day itself was a present, wrapped in the silvery mist that lay along the river and tied loosely with the rays of sunshine that filtered through the low clouds.

Maidey had no such feeling. To her the day was little different from any other except that she had not gone to Canterbury to work and that she had Kent with her.

It was a cold day. Ice had been forming in marshy places and along the edge of the river the past three nights, and it would take more than a few hours of pale sunlight to penetrate the chill that lay over the land. But even if it was to be a day of work for her, they would be in a comfortable house and they would have a chance to eat well. The coal she would save from not having to keep her own cottage warm all day would amount to something. She did not relish the thought of another stove and unfamiliar equipment, but she knew she could cope as she had on other occasions.

She had tried to learn from Kent what Mr. John Rivven was like. That he was an artist and therefore to be distrusted she knew. In fairness she reminded herself that she had never really known an artist, but she had known a writer and she felt them to be similar. They both worked on paper. There could not be a great deal of difference between the one who used color and the one who used words. She had asked Kent repeatedly about his new acquaintance but she got no clear answers. Almost immediately Kent would start talking about ancient people or mulberry trees or things that were as remote from Maidey's mind as the washing she had done the previous fortnight.

Uncertain as she felt about Mr. John Rivven, she had a certainty about Kent which she had not felt in a long time. He had seemed somehow different the last few weeks. Maidey could not put it just to the fact that he was growing. She had said that before at various stages of his life. Now, there seemed to be a reason for his growing inwardly as well as in inches and pounds. It was as if he were reaching toward something he might one day be able to grasp.

As they approached Beekeep, Maidey was satisfied that the goose was already doing nicely. A succulent aroma was on the air, even before the cottage door was opened. The man who stood in the doorway greeted Kent warmly. Maidey momentarily lost her decorum when he greeted her the same way. There was such pleasantness in his voice, such an honest welcome in his smile, that Maidey found herself smiling as she took his outstretched hand. Then decorum returned as she stepped over the threshold into the house.

"You've been very kind to my boy, Mr. Rivven. I'm pleased to be able to do something for you."

"Let me take your coat, Mrs. Conner, and yours, too, Kent." John Rivven opened a closet door and hung the coats side by side, Maidey's thin black Sunday best and Kent's, whose frayed cuffs had been neatly mended.

"It's a bit raw today in spite of the sun," John Rivven went on. "Won't you warm yourself by the fire for a few minutes?"

Maidey shook her head. "Thank you, sir, but I won't. I'd best be on my way to the kitchen to see to the bird and to all else that needs doing." Maidey took the paper bag she had been carrying and looked expectantly in the direction of the kitchen.

"I'll show you," John Rivven said as he went down the short passage. "I think you'll find everything in order, Mrs. Conner. Tessa has been in and out several times this morning and she'll be back again presently."

"Very good, sir."

The kitchen door closed behind them. Kent stared at it, then he went into the sitting room to stand before the fire. The string and paper that had wrapped the day had fallen away. Now it was his to live in while it lasted, to keep as long as it could be remembered.

The oak log that Kent had helped drag down from the path high up on the Downs lay against the back of the hearth. It held the flames of smaller logs and helped send their heat out into the room. A thousand years the tree from which the log had come had been growing, and it was still growing. The log would be the warm core of Christmas for a household of people. If it was banked with ash at night and not encouraged to blaze up during the day, it might smolder on for the whole twelve days of Christmas.

As many days as there are months in the year, Kent thought as he watched the fire and held out his hands to catch some of its warmth against his palms, then he went on to wonder. If the months were cherished, as the log would have to be for a fullness of burning, each one could be lit with a memory of the twelve days. The thought of extending the warmth of one period of time through a whole year was exciting to Kent. Next time Miss Hinshaw asked for a composition he would try to find a way to tell the story of a yule log whose twelve-day burning tipped with flame the months of the year as they came in their orderly sequence.

The cottage door opened and closed and Tessa entered the room. Her cheeks, red from running in the wind, made her dark eyes look darker than ever. She nodded to Kent and they exchanged "Happy Christmas" greetings, then she hurried into the kitchen to see what she could do toward dinner. John Rivven called to Kent from the passage, suggesting a walk so the womenfolk could have the house to themselves.

Promptly at one-thirty they sat down at the big table at the kitchen end of the sitting room. Cleared of books and lamp and magazines, it was now laid with a white cloth. Silver and glass caught light from the sun that came in through the small-paned windows. A bowl of fruit served as a centerpiece. Plates that had been warmed in the oven waited at each place for all that would be put on them. In books Kent had read about such a table. He had often tried to imagine what it would be like to sit down at one; if Tessa had ever dreamed of such a table, she had never expected to see one.

Maidey came in from the kitchen bearing a silver platter on which was the bird, roasted a golden brown. She set it down before their host. Her cheeks were flushed from bending over the stove; wisps of her hair were escaping around her face. "There now," she said with a smile that looked as if it might never fade.

The rest of the meal was brought in to take its place on the table. Maidey laid the carving tools on either side of the silver platter, the two-pronged fork and the knife sharpened so that the thin edge of the blade shone. She went to the kitchen to take off her apron and push back the rebellious strands of hair. Returning to the table, she slipped into the chair that was waiting for her.

Kent gazed at the golden bird, the small mountain of mashed potatoes, the steaming dish of boiled onions, the brown gravy, the bowl of bread sauce, the sticks of celery, and the deep red currant jelly. He looked across the table at his mother, feeling an immense surge of pride and love that she had done something so beautiful.

"And to think there's plum pudding to come!" Tessa breathed, her voice scarcely above a whisper.

John Rivven glanced up from his carving to look from Tessa to Kent. "You'd think you two had never seen a Christmas dinner before."

Neither Kent nor Tessa returned his glance, but each looked at the other and smiled. There were some things that were best kept to oneself.

Maidey said, "If the knife needs a bit more of an edge, Mr. Rivven, I'll take it back to the kitchen."

"Nothing needs anything, Mrs. Conner," he replied. "Everything is done to perfection." After the prayer, he said, "Here's to your good appetite!" and the first plate served was handed to her.

Sunlight no longer filtered into the room when they got up from the table. Maidey and Tessa removed the dishes to the kitchen while John Rivven stirred up the fire and Kent brought in an armful of wood from the stack near the old beehive.

"Would you say it was time for the lamp, sir?" Maidey asked.

"Not for a little while yet, Mrs. Conner. Here, do come and sit down by the fire."

"I'd best tend to the kitchen, sir."

"Oh, not yet, please!" He placed his hand on the back of a chair to gesture her to it. "Lighting-up time will be soon enough for the dishes."

Tessa, standing by a window, noticed one of John Rivven's sketchbooks lying open on a table. "Kent," she exclaimed, at the sketch that caught her eye, "isn't that you?"

He stood beside her and gazed at the picture. "Mmm," he agreed, "and the last of the herons."

John Rivven took the book and laid it on Maidey's lap, then he sat down in the other chair by the fire. "Tell me, would you recognize your son, Mrs. Conner?"

Maidey looked at the sketch, seeing a boy lost against an immensity of sky and a single heron pursuing its way. She stared, trying to see some resemblance between the boy and the Kent she knew. "Can't say as I do, sir, though I'm sure it is a very fine picture. Mightn't it be any boy at all?"

"Seeing is highly individual. What we see is really not nearly so important as what it does to us."

"I wouldn't know about that," Maidey commented politely.

John Rivven stretched his legs out until the toes of his shoes touched the ashes of the fire. "I'd be glad to have you look at the sketches in the book, Maidey, if you'd like."

"Thank you, sir, I would like to do just that."

Turning the pages of the sketchbook carefully, Maidey saw herons in many positions—on their nests, fishing along the river, flying singly or in groups over the familiar landmarks of the village or the wide reaches of the countryside. Most of the drawings were pencil sketches, but at the end of the book were several loose pages of water colors which had been more carefully done from the sketches. Maidey, aware that everyone else in the room was peacefully resting or peacefully occupied, held the colored pictures in her hands and studied them closely.

She saw a tall blue heron standing motionless in the reeds along the river on his long, stiltlike legs. His head was drawn back between his hunched-up shoulders. His keen, sharp beak protruded from the gray feathers of his breast and looked ready to dart in the direction of some hapless prey. His round eyes were hard and intent. They were watching for movement in the weedy shallows at his feet, yet they looked as if they might with equal intent scan the wide sky. In a fraction of a second, with a lightninglike movement, he might take off, or he might remain as he was, immobile, for an hour.

Maidey turned to the next drawing. Its suddenness made her draw in her breath, for quicker than the eye could see it, the heron had uncoiled his long neck, shot his great beak down into the weeds and water and lifted it again, for the picture showed him with his beak tilted to the sky and from it dangled a kicking frog. Maidey turned to another drawing and breathed more easily. Now the heron had risen in flight from the river, huge wings were outspread, thin legs were trailing behind. She saw, almost as if with the glassy glitter of the heron's eye, the wide view that he commanded.

Realizing that Mr. Rivven was watching her, Maidey closed the book. "Now that's an odd thing," she said, "but I've lived in Chilham all my life and I've never thought much of the herons. They come in the spring and they go in the autumn and that's the way it is."

"Not odd at all, Mrs. Conner. The sun rises in the morning and sets at night and with a good many people that's the way it is."

"But, sir, if you don't mind my saying so, you've made them so handsome. I've never seen them in the way you've drawn them."

"Most of us don't ever see things as they really are until our attention is attracted to them, then what we see becomes a part of us at the point where we can give it meaning."

"I never thought herons were beautiful until I saw them in Uncle John's drawings," Tessa said.

"That's because beauty is capable of many definitions. Herons are interesting to draw with those long thin legs that look so ungainly when they're standing on their nests and so purposeful when they stream out in flight. But quite aside from their physical structure which suits their needs so well is what they symbolize."

"The returning year," Kent said. "Spring and all that."

John Rivven nodded. "That's the real beauty! The heron is part of an ancient pattern given us by the Creator, that renewal of life, that cycle of seasons, which assures us that life goes on and that all will be well in Chilham."

"As long as life goes on and people eat Christmas dinners there'll be washing up to do," Maidey said as she rose from her chair. "Come along, Tessa."

Reluctantly Tessa rose and followed Maidey to the kitchen.

"Let us know, Mrs. Conner, if we can lend a hand," John Rivven called after them.

"Thank you, sir, but this is women's work. You and Kent must excuse us for an hour." The door closed behind them.

"Well, Kent, I suppose we can find some men's work to do. There's a bit of wood outside that could well be sawed into fireplace lengths."

They worked together for an hour, then each brought in an armful of the newly cut wood and laid it on the hearth in readiness for later burning. John Rivven stirred the red coals of the fire and put on a new log that flamed and crackled, filling the dusky room with quick shifting shadows and sudden jagged edges of light. They stood with their backs to the blaze, watching the leaping shadows on the opposite wall, like herons unlimbering themselves for flight.

"I wonder," Kent said, almost as much to himself as to the man beside him, "why it is that the herons keep coming back to Chilham when the fishing and the nesting might be just as good some other place."

"They know they belong. Isn't that enough?"

Kent nodded. He agreed, and yet he could not have explained the feeling that was groping toward reality within him; but he knew, with a comforting assurance, that Uncle John would not ask him any more.

And he did not. He merely commented, "You've got what the herons have, Kent, one country where your ties are, where you belong, another for your wingspan."

Kent turned around and stared at the fire—at the new wood burning briskly and the blackened shape of the back log. He did not want to look at John Rivven, for the voice that had spoken to him just then was not like the voice of the man with whom he had shared tea and gone back into history and sawed up wood. It was the voice of another man, someone he could remember only as a voice reading aloud to him at night before sleep came. It was someone he thought he had never known.

The room was silent. Beyond the closed door were the muted voices of the two who were working in the kitchen, the sound of water running, of dishes being stacked on shelves, of cutlery being put away in drawers, a catch of laughter and then an exchange of words. In the sitting room there was only the crackling of the fire and the stealthy creeping of dusk as the short December day began to draw to its close.

Kent knew now why he had felt that the day itself was the present to be unwrapped, for during the passing of the hours he had found the gift that was for him alone. What was true for the herons was true for him. He belonged to Chilham, to this corner of earth where birds returned and mulberries grew, where invaders had pushed all before them and pilgrims had told their beads and their tales. He breathed a long deep breath. It was an odd sensation to feel suddenly, unquestionably, that he belonged in the place where he had lived all his life.

"Uncle John, I—" Kent began, then the door from the kitchen opened and Mrs. Conner came in. Tessa followed with a tray. The pleasurable necessities of afternoon tea were upon them.

After tea Kent and Tessa went out for a walk. John Rivven slid deep into his chair, pointing his feet toward the fire. Maidey leaned back in her chair. A comfortable sense of well-being put her at ease. She told herself that she had no reason to feel as she did in the house of a person who had employed her to do a piece of work and whom she would, like as not, never see again; but she excused herself with the thought that she had little enough ease in her life and she might as well take what had come to her on this particular day. The softly lit, fire-warmed room was a pleasant interlude and the presence of the other human being in it was completely undemanding. Gazing into the fire, she contented herself with her own thoughts.

John Rivven watched her, seeing all he needed to see through half-shut eyes. He longed for a pencil in hand and a sketchbook on his knee, but he knew quite well how alarmed she would have been had he asked permission to draw her. The moment was blissfully mellow, compounded of the good dinner, the sense of friendliness, and the day's peace. He would do nothing to jeopardize it. Observing her carefully, he felt that he could depend on the discipline of his memory to give back to him what he was seeing now when he had a sheet of paper before him and was holding a pencil.

She was not beautiful, but then, as he loved to say, beauty was capable of many definitions. Her brow was too high, perhaps, her nose a bit too long; but she was good-looking and as true to type as a piece of architecture. Her plain, honest face, with the color in her cheeks heightened from her work in the kitchen and now from the fire, was the face of one who had not asked much of life. He doubted if she had even been given much by life; what she had, she had discovered or made for herself. She must have come to terms with life almost as soon as she had learned how to read and write, for her attitude of acceptance was so evident; but it was an acceptance within whose confines she had found composure.

Her face was unlined, not entirely because the years had not had time to do their etching but because of that center of calm she possessed, something that was as distinct a part of her as her smooth, fair hair. Married to the routines of life as she had been, she must have moved to them without resistance, for what might have seemed submission in some people was apparently voluntary with her. Narrow as her way of duty had probably been, within it she had discovered her happiness. He wondered if she had always worked for other people, in their homes, with their belongings, or if there had ever been a time when she had worked for herself.

Whatever the work, around it and herself she had built a protective wall of dignity and decorum.

She was like a woman in an old Dutch painting, he decided, quietly occupied with some household task, doing that of which she was capable with the tools at hand, and doing it with decent pride. The world was filled with people able and equipped to get ahead, striving for mastery, pushing others out of their way, he told himself; but there were still some like Maidey Conner who found humble work a holy thing. Studying her face and bringing Kent's to mind, he could see little resemblance between them; but the pale smooth hair was the same and each had the same strong capable pair of hands.

He imagined her in a dozen different poses—on her knees while she cleaned a grate in the early morning, a heavy wool sweater drawn close at the neck for warmth; standing by a kitchen stove and stirring a custard with a wooden spoon; leaning against a table as she poured milk into glasses or cut slices from a loaf of bread; working in a garden, her muscled arms as capable of turning over the earth as they were of turning out a room. She might speak with a certain exclusiveness of "woman's work," but she was one who had done "man's work" too for a good part of her life.

He saw her as she was now in the neat black dress that because it was of no particular style was free from fashion, with that small shining nutmeg around her neck dangling from the wide-linked dog chain that must have been bought at an ironmonger's. It was her only ornament, it, and the band of her wedding ring. He saw her in the striped overall that she most likely wore as a uniform in her daily work. He saw her in the generous white apron she had brought with her to wear while cooking the dinner and taken off before she had sat down at the table. Seeing her as he did, it was always in some relation to what she was wearing. Her clothes were as much a part of her being as feathers were for the herons.

Maidey had not felt so happy in a long time, or so rested in spite of the long walk and the work in a strange kitchen. Leaning back in her chair, she had closed her eyes for a few minutes as there was no reason to keep them open. Perhaps she dozed off, but it made no difference for when she opened her eyes again everything was exactly the same. She turned her head a trifle to look at Mr. Rivven, relieved to see that his eyes were closed.

She did not want to do anything to disturb him, but her hands felt empty with no work in them. She thought of the mending basket in her own cottage, filled and waiting for the odd moments in her evenings. Mr. Rivven must have a mending basket which she could apply herself to. She let her eyes roam around the room, but they did not see any such basket. Then she remembered that it was Christmas Day and settled back in her chair again. She would not sew on Christmas any more than she would on Sunday.

"Are you quite comfortable, Mrs. Conner?"

Startled at the sound of his voice, Maidey exclaimed, "Yes, indeed, sir. The fire is a pleasant thing, but I expect we should be going soon. I hope Kent won't be too long."

"They've probably stopped in for a bit at Tessa's. I asked her to fetch me some eggs for my breakfast, if her mother can spare any." He paused, then went on, "I'm not really used to being sir'd, Mrs. Conner."

There was an answering pause. In the silence a new world might have been born, an old one might have prevailed.

"No one ever calls me anything but Maidey, Mr. Rivven." The emphasis on the *mister* was slight but unmistakable.

"Tell me something about yourself, Maidey."

"What would you like to know, Mr. Rivven?"

"Oh, where you live, what you do."

"We live in Chilham and I do general housework in Canterbury five days a week. I've been in my present place going on four years. Before that I cooked in a restaurant."

"Have you always lived in Chilham?"

"Yes, except for a week in London. That was when I was married. And I've been to Ramsgate for more than one weekend, and to Walmer Sands."

"You are a widow?"

"Yes."

There was a long pause, a pause that might have grown into a longer silence had John Rivven not broken it.

"Tell me something about Kent's father."

"He was an American. An Air Force man attached to the base at Lympne. He liked his work, but he always said that when his time was up he wanted to go back to being a writer. That was why he took such a fancy to Chilham. Then one day it was all over. He's buried in the new part of the churchyard."

"An accident?"

"Yes."

The words came to an end as the experience had come to an end. Maidey gave no indication that it had been difficult to relate the story of her life. She had been asked a series of questions; she had responded with the facts.

"You were happy?"

"Yes, indeed"—there was a moment of hesitation—"while it lasted."

"What was he like, Maidey, your husband?"

"He was a very neat-appearing gentleman, Mr. Rivven, and very well spoken. He was a great reader. He used to read aloud to Kent. Sometimes when I'd hear him the words sounded like another language, but the boy listened as if he understood. He wasn't more than three years old in those days," Maidey added with a note of pride.

"Do you still have the books?"

She shook her head. "I kept a few things for a while, then I sold everything. Kent was very ill when he was seven years old; that's why he's a year behind at school. I had to sell everything to help pay the doctor's bills."

"I'm sorry, Maidey, very sorry."

"There was nothing I particularly wanted to remember."

"But Kent—"

"He couldn't remember his father at all. When he started in at school he called himself 'Mr. Nobody.' He'd taken a liking to the name and—" Maidey stopped suddenly. "Now, that's odd! But I haven't heard him call himself that for a long time."

"Your husband had relatives in America?"

"He used to speak about a brother in a place called Virginia, and his father was living at the time. They wrote to me after it happened, but I didn't keep up the correspondence."

"Perhaps it seemed better not to recall the past."

"What good would it have done us?"

John Rivven stood up to stir the fire and lay another log on the bed of coals, then he sat down again in the deep chair and reached his feet to the edge of the ash. "I wonder what good it does the herons when they're nesting here in Chilham to think back to Africa—the frog-filled marshes of the Nile, the reedy coves of the Mediterranean. What good does it do any of us to recall something that has passed?"

Maidey did not answer, for he had not asked her a question. He had merely made a statement. She settled back in her chair wishing Kent would return so they could go home. But she was not as comfortable as she had been, though the fire was as warm and the chair as easy. She did not like the pricking needle of disquiet that had somehow worked itself into the room, into the space between the two chairs drawn up to the fire.

"Better not to remember the past," she told herself. Was it better? Better than what? Better than if the past had not been? The words knocked at her mind like fingers on a long-closed door and she knew quite well that the knocking would not cease until she had found the handle with which she could open the door. She sighed.

"What is ahead for Kent, Maidey?"

"He'll go to the county school at Chatham next year. When he's sixteen he can go to work."

"What kind of work?"

"I'd like him to learn a trade while he's working, but it makes no matter as long as it's a steady job. There's plenty of them about. Many a shopkeeper in Canterbury needs a delivery boy and Kent might in time work into the business. That is, if he doesn't get notions."

"Tessa has notions, Maidey, did you know that?"

Maidey's eyes widened as she turned to him. "Whatever could they be and wherever would she get them? She's a nice-mannered girl and neat in her ways, but she's not much more than a gypsy child even though her mother does keep a few hens to help out—"

"She has a strange rare gift of compassion, Maidey, and she seems able to take the whole world into her thinking. What she'll do with it, or how, or when, no one can say, but it would be a pity if her education did not go on beyond the county school. Her parents realize that; hard-working folk as they are, they know that among their brood of ducklings a swan was somehow hatched."

"Education," Maidey repeated, "that's what Kent's father always said he wanted for the boy."

"Then I suppose it's up to you to help him get the best education he can."

"All I want for Kent is that he'll learn how to earn a day's honest pay and be true to those who love him."

"The county school won't take Kent far enough, Maidey, or will it?"

To that question there was no easily given answer. Again the tap of fingers sounded on the inner door. But even had Maidey, in courtesy, been able to give an answer there was no time. Voices could be heard outside the cottage. The door was opened and a sharp current of night air flowed into the room as Tessa and Kent came in.

Tessa carried a basket of eggs which she set carefully on the table, then as carefully delivered the message with which she had been instructed. "My mum says she'll be glad to come up and get your breakfasts while Mrs. Talbot is away."

"Is your housekeeper to be away for long?" Maidey asked, quick to realize the helplessness of a man alone.

"I've given her the twelve days of Christmas," John Rivven said casually, then went on to explain. "She really only wanted to have a week but I decided that when Christmas was concerned full measure was the rule."

"And who's to get your dinner at night?" Maidey asked.

"Mum, Mum—" Kent looked at her eagerly.

"I'll make out all right, Maidey. I really can do for myself when I have to."

"Oh, Mum, please—" Kent begged.

Maidey hesitated, then she spoke out. "Mr. Rivven, I'd be pleased to come in evenings after I get back from Canterbury. It wouldn't be until after six, but if Tessa could get the vegetables washed and the meat in, I'd be on hand to do the rest."

Good-bys were soon being said, but not until a plan for the ensuing days had been arrived at. Kent gave the back log a friendly glance, wondering if it would burn through to the twelfth day.

It was dark and there were no stars shining when they started home. Tessa walked with Kent and his mother as far as her cottage. When she said good-by she kissed Maidey impulsively, then turned and ran quickly into the darkness. They stood still to watch her go through the door of her cottage, then to watch it close behind her.

Maidey sighed. "I declare, but I love that girl as if I were her parent!"

Kent felt that he could say the same about John Rivven, but he kept the words to himself.

There were lights burning in many of the houses as they walked through the village Square. In the warm glow that streamed out from the Woolpack Inn, Maidey saw Kent in a new way. She exclaimed, almost in surprise, "Kent, you're up to my shoulders now! You'll be out of that suit before I've saved up enough to buy you a new one."

The prospect of a new suit was a pleasing one to Kent and it did not seem so far distant as once it had. "If you cook Uncle John's dinners for the next eleven days, he may pay you enough to buy me a suit and a dress for yourself."

Maidey shook her head. "I'll not take money for anything I do for him."

The Ash Is Still Warm

7

The log did last until the twelfth day. It burned through in the center by the fourth night and fell apart in two pieces. One piece was used as a back log, and when it was gone the other was put in its place. Carefully banked with ashes each night and fed with wood during the day, the fire had been the glowing center of the Christmas season. Something else had lasted, as well, and that was the cheer that had made four people into a family with the bachelor cottage of Beekeep as their rendezvous.

Kent had never known such a holiday, not only for its friendliness and fun and food but for the sense of importance given him. Each day before leaving for Canterbury, his mother wrote out a list of duties for him to perform at Beekeep—cleaning shoes, polishing brass, scrubbing floors were some of them. Kent had been amazed at the number and variety that his mother could discover.

Many of the tasks did not seem either necessary or important to him, but that made no difference to Maidey. She explained to Kent that it was the care a gentleman required and they were only things she would do herself if she could get there before it was time to devote herself to the evening meal. On her free Thursday she put aside the needs of her own cottage and made up to Beekeep what she had not had time to do the other days and could not entrust to Kent. Kitchen shelves were wiped over and every window in the cottage washed.

John Rivven, coming back from a long walk with Tessa and Kent, smiled and shook his head at Maidey as she finished her work on the last windowpane. "Maidey, Maidey, you shouldn't spend so much time on my windows!"

"That's for me to say, Mr. John," she replied, flicking her cloth in the breeze. "I'm taking care of your cottage this week, and if I think the windows need washing it's up to me to give it to them. There now, they do look nice!" She stood back and surveyed her work.

"They sparkle," Tessa said, then she pointed to one of the tiny upstairs windows that peeped out from under the overhanging tiles. The sun flashing on the panes of glass made them dance with light. "They're like the eyes of a happy person."

"I suppose windows are like eyes," Maidey agreed, "and a man who does the work that Mr. John does is entitled to look through clean ones."

There had been work for Tessa as well as for Kent during the days, Maidey had seen to that, but there had been hours and hours in which they had been free to follow their own pursuits. Never had Kent had so much time for reading or so many books to read as those he found for himself on the shelves at Beekeep. Every evening at seven o'clock they had sat down to dinner, all four of them, and when dinner was over and the washing-up done they gathered by the fire. Maidey had discovered the mending basket with enough in it to keep her hands busy while the others read or talked together, or listened to stories told them by their host. One memorable evening he had spent sketching them.

"Don't feel you have to do anything special, Maidey," he had said when she ceased her sewing and sat stiffly in the chair with her hands folded awkwardly in her lap. "I like you all as you are, doing something natural. That's how I like to find the herons."

So the time had gone—day after work-filled, adventure-filled day until there were twelve in all, and through them the great oak log burned and broke apart, then burned again until on the twelfth night it was reduced to a bed of coals. The whole huge hearth held its warmth, from the blackened bricks to those that made the outer frame for the room. A hand held near or laid on the bricks could take the warmth to itself.

To Kent, sitting on the floor with his knees hunched up to his chin and gazing into the fire, it was a cause for wonder that the yule log had lasted. To Maidey, sitting straight-backed in her chair, it was only what was to be expected of a good-sized piece of wood. There would be warmth for half the night in the bed of coals it had left, and even by morning the ash would still be warm. She had cleaned enough and grated as many hearths to know that. Her knitting needles clicked as she approached the heel of the second sock of a pair she was making. Having come to the end of what was in the mending basket and not wanting to be idle, she had started something she knew she could finish in a given time.

With the morning, life would be different for each one of them. Kent and Tessa would be back at school. Mrs. Talbot would have returned to take charge of Beekeep. Maidey would have only one place of work.

"What will you be doing tomorrow, Uncle John?"

"Packing."

Tessa and Kent made startled exclamations, repeating the word in questioning tones as if its meaning was obscure.

It was Maidey who calmly asked, "You're going away then?"

"Yes, in a few days, perhaps a week. I've no set time. I'm going to Africa for the sun, and some sketching, and to find the herons in their winter grounds."

"Will you be gone long?"

He shook his head. "I'll be back with the herons, or a few days before. I wouldn't miss their arrival for anything."

Kent breathed again with relief. That would not be more than five weeks, or six at the most. What happened during that time he should be able to remember to tell Uncle John about on his return.

"How do they know when to come?" Tessa asked. "How is it they can arrive always on St. Valentine's Day?"

"Oh, they are sometimes a day or two ahead or behind that date," John Rivven answered, "but they keep so close to schedule that they've built a tradition for themselves—sign of spring, and symbol for well-being."

"There's so much in a year that often isn't well," Maidey murmured.

"True, and yet I have a suspicion that if you weighed in a scale the good with the ill for a given year, it would be the good that would tip the scale."

There was no answering that and, what was more, Maidey had come to the turning of the heel. She removed herself from the conversation in the necessity of counting stitches.

"But how do they know when to come?" Tessa insisted. "They haven't any calendars the way we have."

"They have what went before all calendars—God fitted them into nature's plan and linked them with the orderly procedure, like the tides in their ebb and flow, the stars in their courses. It's said that a restlessness begins to come over the herons when the sun travels a higher arc and the hours of daylight lengthen. An urgency seizes them to return to the place where they have nested before, or if they are yearlings, the place where they hatched and where they may nest again in safety.

"The herons could go some place else if they were obliged to—if men cut down their nesting trees or changed the course of the river that feeds them and their tradition became broken; but this place, this heronry at Chilham, is the birthright of this particular flock. This is where they feel at home in the world. They know what they need and, year after year, they return to the place that can give it to them. It is their God-given instinct. What we try to define in a complicated way is very simple to them: they yield themselves to the awakening year and move forward with it."

"It's like a pattern, isn't it?" Tessa asked. "A pattern much bigger than they are but which they can fit themselves into."

"Exactly, and the herons have been fitting themselves into it not just for centuries but for ages. Trouble or misfortune may diminish their numbers, but given time they bring them up again. They take what exists for them—the highways of the air for traveling, the high tops of the trees for nesting, the waterways for feeding—and they live very full lives."

"They don't all come back every year, do they, Uncle John?" Kent asked.

"No, not all. Some meet with disaster, some succumb to age, and a few every year break away from the flock to find another nesting ground and establish a new tradition."

"What a long, long flight it must be for them, from Africa to Chilham and back again, every year."

"It is, Tessa, more than two thousand miles by the shortest route and over sea and land, but they prepare themselves for it for weeks, feeding heavily, going on longer and longer flights; and when the instinct to migrate sweeps through them they take off with strong sure wings and bodies fit for the ordeal. I've watched them many times in the early autumn, seized by the need that lifts them onto the air, rising, spiraling, their wings beating in that measured effortless way they have. The sound of their voices as they get into position has even spilled down from the sky to reach my ears. They'll swing in an easy circle, always getting higher and higher, then their lines will straighten somewhat as they set their wings for what almost appears to be a slow drift southward. And then, they've gone beyond my sight!"

"So high, so very high!"

John Rivven nodded, his admiration of the herons one with his affection for them. "Once long ago, the Roman poet Virgil said that the herons had such strong wings that they could fly above the storm clouds where the air was always clear. That's the reason why a heron became a heraldic symbol. A knight would choose it for his coat of arms to signify a man who could rise above misfortunes and the attacks of his enemies as a heron rises above the storm."

Tessa was puzzled. "How can they ever see where they're going if they rise so high?"

"Tell me, Tessa, how much farther do you see when you walk along the ridge of the Downs than when you walk in the meadows along the river?"

"Oh, Uncle John, what a silly question! Much more. On a clear day, from the Downs, I think I can see to the Channel."

"Even so with the herons. The higher they rise, the farther they see, and as all migrating birds do they keep the horizon at the level of their eyes. It's simple fact, as you have told me, that as one goes up, the miles below decrease in size and more miles come into view. The herons have their way of recognizing directives on their course as you would have if you walked by field the six miles to Canterbury."

"You'd almost think you'd been a heron, Uncle John," Kent said.

"Sometimes I almost think I have been," he agreed; "I've thought myself into those feathered bodies so often."

Maidey, hearing John Rivven's voice as it went on, only half heard what he was saying. She was nearing the toe and had to count frequently, but she was fully aware of what was going on as he answered the promptings of the two who sat on the floor looking up at him. It made her think of summer days on the sands at Walmer when Kent was only a little thing building his castles and wading at the sea's creeping edge. Her whole attention was taken up in watching him and though the other Kent, stretched on the sand beside her, might be talking or reading to her something he had written, she only half heard him for her mind was on the boy.

There were so many things that she had not thought of or wanted to let into her mind for such a long time. Now she found it pleasant to live back in those days when everything had been different. They would not come again, she told herself as she narrowed in for the toe of the sock, just as last spring's flowers would not come again, but there was no harm in recalling them.

She finished the toe and broke off the wool, then threaded a needle and wove the wool back and forth to secure it. She folded the sock and laid it with the other, glad that she had been able to complete the pair before the twelve days were up. Maidey knew she would miss coming to Beekeep every night. It had been something to take care of a man again, even if she had known all along that the work was not to last. It had made her feel more alive than she had felt in years.

"Uncle John, tell us about the first time you ever saw a heron," asked Kent.

"Oh, that's a good tale," he said, laughing, "and it doesn't go back too far either."

The easy voice launched into a story.

Maidey turned her head to watch him as he spoke, glad that his attention was absorbed so she could be unobserved. He was an odd sort of person, far too kind and friendly to be living alone. If anyone had told her as short a time as two weeks ago that she could have been comfortable in mind and body for ten whole evenings and two whole days as she had been in Mr. John's house, she would not have believed it possible.

She would have chided herself for what seemed like taking a liberty of comfort had it not been for the boy. Kent was happier than he had been in many months, and he wasn't growing just in height now. He was growing sideways a bit. It was hard on his clothes but better for him in the end. And it was good for Kent to have Tessa, almost as good as if he had a sister of his own.

But John Rivven puzzled her. He seemed to need so little—a clean house, a good meal every day, time safeguarded for his work, and young people to take an interest in. Maidey supposed Mrs. Talbot was kind to him, but you could never be sure. He was a very well-informed gentleman; she realized that from the way he could talk on and on as if all the books he had ever read were in his head, and she was willing to admit that he was a fine artist. He made the herons look more natural to her than the birds themselves, and his drawings of the countryside were all of places that she could easily find herself in.

She could not follow him when he got going on ancient history, but then he had admitted that he could not follow her when she turned the heel of a sock or set a Queen pudding before him at the table. "Everyone to his own skill," he had said more than once; and Maidey, instead of feeling conscious of the lack of book learning in her, was proud of what she could do. Watching him as he talked, she wondered what it would be like if this were to go on not just for twelve days but for twelve months.

He looked up suddenly and caught her glance. Maidey dropped her eyes, but there was now no work in her lap on which she might fasten her attention. She leaned forward to pick up the socks she had laid on the floor and as she did the light caught on the silver nutmeg and made a momentary flashing.

"That's an interesting thing that you wear, Maidey," John Rivven said. "I've wondered about it all these days. It has a meaning, I'm sure, the way my pictures have though I'm the only one who ever knows it."

Kent flashed a smile at his mother, as sudden and brilliant in its way as the light had been on the nutmeg. "Shall we tell him, Mum?"

Maidey nodded. "You may, Kent, if you wish."

"England is inside it, Uncle John. English earth from the path on the Downs where the little ancient people fought and the pilgrims stopped to talk. *English earth as much as either hand may rightly clutch.*"

John Rivven was smiling as he continued,

> *"In the taking of it breathe*
> *Prayer for all who lie beneath—"*

"Then you know it too?"

"What Englishman doesn't?"

"Where is it, Mr. John; what is it from?" Maidey asked, quite forgetful of her momentary confusion. "I've heard it said, and so has Kent, but we can get no farther with it than the first few lines."

John Rivven got up from his chair and went toward the bookcase. "It's one of Rudyard Kipling's poems."

John Rivven put the book in Kent's hands. "Take it home with you, Kent, and read it to your mother. The book is yours to keep. I've something for you, Tessa. It's a flashlight to help you find your way at night." He took up a narrow box from the table and handed it to Tessa.

"And I've a pair of socks for you, Mr. John," said Maidey as she gave him her handwork. "They should fit for I matched them to a pair of yours that I was mending."

"We seem to be starting Christmas all over again instead of ending it, and that's as it should be. That's what the herons keep saying—good always comes again."

Soon they were standing in the little passage, putting on their coats, saying good-by to each other and making their plans to meet soon after the heron's return in February.

"The next fine day," John Rivven reminded them. There was no need of a calendar for that.

Kent, holding his book under his arm, went down the path with Tessa who flashed her new light excitedly ahead of them. Maidey went to the kitchen for a moment to assure herself that everything had been left exactly as Mrs. Talbot would like to find it.

"If you've had the same housekeeper since you've been living here, I wouldn't want her upset because a stranger had been taking care of your house, Mr. John."

He held the thin black coat for Maidey to slide her arms into. "Maidey, I'm beginning to think Mrs. Talbot won't know she's been away. Between you and Tessa and Kent, the cottage looks polished to perfection and no one can say that I haven't been well fed."

"It's been a pleasure to do what I could for you."

"Has it, Maidey?"

"Yes, indeed, Mr. John. And if you like—after your return—anytime—" She paused, then laughed at herself. "Now, I mustn't go saying that! When your Mrs. Talbot is back she won't fancy having another woman around." She turned and started down the step. "But Mr. John, if you're ever left in the lurch, so to speak, I'll be glad to come and do for you anytime."

"Maidey—"

She turned to look at him.

"Wait, please. I want to tell you something. I want to say something to you."

Maidey waited.

Far ahead down the lane the voices of Kent and Tessa could be heard, the flashing of the light could be seen, like a will-o'-the-wisp on a winter's night. John Rivven reached for words and, before Maidey's quiet decorum, failed to find them. If he could take color and use it on a canvas he could say what he was feeling, but that would be his way not hers. For her, words must be clear and precise, like the list of duties for the day or the courses for a meal.

"Wait," he put his hand on her arm, "you can't go like this. I must say something to you, something that's been uppermost within me for days. Maidey, Maidey, could you ever bring yourself to care for me, even a little?"

"For Kent's sake?" she asked quickly.

He shook his head. "For mine alone, because I've come to care for you, Maidey. It was something I thought would never happen to me again. I thought my work was everything in my life, but now I know it isn't. It's as real to me as yours is to you, as Kent is to you, but Maidey—it isn't everything now."

She looked at him steadily, eyes meeting eyes. "Thank you, Mr. John, but I once did care for a gentleman and I do not think a feeling like that can come again."

There was such finality to her words that he dropped his hand from her arm and moved back toward the open door.

"I'll send you a check tomorrow for—for these twelve days."

She moved with a quick step or two toward him. "No, no, you must never do that. I cannot accept money for what I've done for you." She held out her hand to him.

He reached to take it, willing to respect her wishes. Standing there on the doorstep of Beekeep with the raw wind of the January night around them and the lighted cottage behind them, they shook hands.

"Good night, Maidey, please don't say good-by."

"I'll not say good-by, Mr. John. Good night is enough." She turned and walked into the darkness.

He stood in the doorway until the sound of her footsteps had gone into the night, then he closed the door and went back to stand by his hearth whose only warmth now came from a bed of coals. For the first time in the years he had lived alone, the cottage seemed empty and silent. He felt an aching sense of loneliness as if something had slipped from his hands that he might have been holding if he had the skill to grasp it.

Maidey did not overtake Tessa and Kent until they had almost reached Tessa's cottage, and then there was time only to say good night. As Maidey and Kent turned to follow the path that would take them back to Chilham, Kent said, "I thought you didn't like artists, Mum."

"Whether he's an artist or not makes no difference to me, Kent," Maidey replied. "He's a man who needs someone to take care of him and I've tried to do my best."

Winter's Hold

8

For a week or more, the glow that had enfolded the holiday season lasted and then it gradually began to disappear. "You can't keep anything forever," Maidey said practically. That it had not been a dream she knew because of the slight sense of disquiet that had entered her mind. She began to wonder if she had done the right thing in spending as much time as she had at Beekeep. In an endeavor to allay her feelings in some way, she devoted herself with passionate attention to her own cottage. Two rooms did not make many demands, but Maidey found release in caring for them.

Winter came down over the countryside in earnest by mid-January, holding the land in a grip of cold. The river Stour froze so that there were many places where it could be crossed on the ice. There were days when snow blew in on a wind from the northeast. The cottages with their red tile roofs looked as if they had gone white-haired during the night. The snow, melting down the tiles, sometimes froze and left a fringe of icicles. Traveling was bad on the roads and people kept to their homes as much as possible. Then, inevitably it seemed, like a counterpart of the cold, illness began to creep through the town. Many people failed to go to work and only half the children were at school.

It was on the coldest of a week of cold days that Kent, reaching home in the afternoon sometime before his mother returned from Canterbury, saw that a letter and a post card had been put under their door. Their cottage was one that the postman was rarely obliged to stop at and the arrival of two communications in one day was an event; that they were from the same person and bore Egyptian stamps only heightened the importance. Kent read his post card over and over and waited impatiently for his mother to return for the news in her letter.

When Maidey got back from work, she picked up the letter and

looked at it. The sight of the known handwriting was disturbing. Maidey was aware that the feeling of uneasiness she thought she had suppressed was fluttering within her again.

"Aren't you going to read it, Mum?"

"All in good time, Kent. We'll have our supper first. If there's bad news in it, it will go better on a full stomach."

"Mum, it couldn't be about anything but the herons and what he's doing. Look at all he said on my card and yours is a letter! He must be having a very exciting time and I'd like to know more about it."

"We shall see." Maidey started to busy herself with preparations for their supper.

When they had finished, she told Kent to get down to his schoolwork while she read the letter. The room was cold around its edges so Kent drew up to the coal fire in the grate, his book open on his knees and his back to his mother. The eagerness burning within him had diminished during supper as his mother's persistent refusal to talk about Uncle John made Kent realize that perhaps she did not want to share the letter with him. He tried to put his mind on his work.

Maidey opened the letter and spread it out flat on the table, close to the lamp. She read it slowly, shaking her head as she read. Then she folded it up, put it back in its envelope, and put the envelope in the pocket of her apron. She got up and crossed the room for her mending basket and brought it back to the table.

Kent, aware of her every movement, turned to ask her the question he could keep within himself no longer. "What does Uncle John say, Mum?"

"He says he's well."

"But what does he say about the herons?"

"He doesn't say anything about the herons, Kent."

Kent stared. Whatever could Uncle John write about then, and such a thick-seeming letter it was, if he didn't tell about the birds he had gone to see! Kent opened his mouth to speak, but at the expression on his mother's face he leaped from his chair and ran to her. "Mum, Mum, what's the matter?" He put his arms around her as if to keep her with him.

"I'm all right, Kent." She put her hand to her head.

"Mum, if you're not feeling well I can stay home from school tomorrow and take care of you. Tessa has been away from school all week taking care of her family. Everyone of them is sick in bed."

Maidey shook her head wearily. "I'll be all right in the morning, Kent; you'd best go back to your work."

And she was.

Sitting at breakfast over their porridge and tea, Maidey had chatted cheerfully with Kent about one thing and another and Kent had gone off to school feeling greatly relieved. The post card with the foreign stamp was in his pocket and he looked forward to showing it to Miss Hinshaw. Perhaps she would tell them all a story about Egypt, and Kent could fill in with a few new bits of information. Even if his mother had read her letter to him, it could not have said much more than he knew already from the card.

Winter always made people act strangely, Kent reflected. Perhaps in the endeavor to keep warm against the severe cold outside and the dampness within the cottages, they huddled themselves into a tightness. Even a coal fire in a grate could not warm people through these days; it would take the sun to do that. School had been going well for Kent the past few weeks and this day was no exception. The self-imposed name "Mr. Nobody" was rarely used now by the children, chiefly because Kent did not use it himself. He could laugh at the way he had thought of himself as a past and present nobody, when it was clear that he was somebody. Everybody was somebody; that was an inescapable fact.

Ever since the Christmas holidays he had been walking home the short way through the Square and the old churchyard, past the new churchyard to the road that led to the Lees. It was not entirely because there was no immediate reason to go by Beekeep Cottage, but because there was an urgent reason to go by a certain stone in the new churchyard. Once he had avoided it; now he could stand beside it and read with pride the words carved on it:

LIEUT. KENT HUGH CONNER

BORN VIRGINIA, U.S.A.

DIED CHILHAM, KENT

English Earth Returned

And the dates of his life span of thirty-two years.

Kent looked at it as if he were looking into the face of a friend. He put his hand on it, conscious of the coolness of the stone. Once he thought he had never known his father. Now he could tell himself that was not true. But he ached to know more about him. What had he looked like? Was he tall? Was Kent like him in any way? Kent tried to imagine him, but the only thing of which he was sure was the sound of a voice.

Standing by the stone and feeling a comforting sense of kinship, Kent said aloud the four verses of Mr. Kipling's poem. He had not been certain that he could say it all the way through, but coming to the last lines without faltering he knew that he had it safely in his mind.

And reveal (which is thy need)
Every man a King indeed!

It was true, as Mr. Kipling said, every man was a king indeed; or a somebody, as Uncle John put it. Kent wondered, when he grew up, if he would be able to write in such a way. His father had wanted to write, and now his father had become a part of history, along with all the others whose lives had built the past. They were the ground from which the present grew and the future flourished. Kent felt himself indebted to them just for having lived, all of them, great men or simple folk.

Of whose life and death is none
Report or lamentation.

He knew that he owed something to them, not an accounting but a carrying on, like a relay race at school when a runner hands another the flag to carry to the goal. It was good to realize that it did not matter about winning the race, only about carrying the flag the apportioned distance and then handing it on to the next runner.

The great bell that told the hours to Chilham rang out over the countryside, four deep full-toned strokes, sharp and echoless in the cold. The sound drew Kent's eyes up to the square tower from which it came. He knew that he should soon go home to get the fire going and have the cottage ready for his mother's return, but his feet were drawn by the sound as his eyes had been and he let them take him to the steps of St. Mary's. The heavy oak door moved easily and Kent stood inside the church. It was cold inside, colder than it had been outdoors, and the light was dim. Somewhere between the sturdy Norman pillars and the oak beams that held the vaulted roof, time was standing still, time was waiting.

Kent walked slowly down one of the side aisles, stopping to read the tablets that commemorated the lives of people who had once made their impress on the everyday world of Chilham. He felt that he belonged to them as they did to him, for they had lived and worked to build the life of which he was now a part. He crossed the center aisle near the altar and started back up the other aisle, stopping by the tablet that memorialized one of the ancient families. His eye passed quickly over the Latin part of the inscription. Beneath the date 1626 that had been cut deep in the stone were the words:

For those outdare the threats of Fate alone
Which are composed of actions, not of stone.

The words seemed to tap him on the shoulder and summon him into the present. Actions! How long had he been dreaming in the church, and before that in the new graveyard! There were tasks waiting for him at home and time would not stand still forever. Walking briskly, he left the church. Lights had come on in several of the houses and the smoke from newly stirred fires was on the air. Kettles would soon be singing from many a hob, as Kent knew theirs should be. People would soon be returning from work in Canterbury and elsewhere.

The sky was low with tattered clouds. Through a rift, one star could be seen, then it was obscured by a slow drifting of the clouds. Kent glanced over his shoulder at the west and tilted his face to the wind, wondering what the weather would be like on the morrow. As he approached his home he was surprised to see that a light was shining from within. It looked inviting, as inviting as had the lights in the other houses he had passed. The light meant that his mother had got home before him, but the bell in St. Mary's had not yet told five o'clock and she was not due back for an hour. What could have happened to bring her home so early?

Kent pushed open the door. The room was empty. The lamp had been lit and was set in its usual place, but his mother was neither standing near it making preparations for supper nor kneeling by the grate to light the fire. The cottage was very cold. The fire had not been laid since morning. Kent, conscious of his failure of duty and alarmed at the empty room, called questioningly, "Mum?" then frantically, "Mum!"

Her answering voice came from upstairs, from the room under the eaves which was used as a storeroom and where Kent had his bed. It was always cold and Maidey rarely went there unless it was to fetch something or to put the hot stone bottle between the sheets before Kent went up to sleep. It was too early for that now, Kent told himself, and what could she be wanting up there that took her so long to get?

Kent went quickly up the narrow stairs and into the small room.

Maidey was sitting on the floor, still wearing her hat and coat. Around her was a confusion of personal belongings, hers as well as Kent's, and before her was an open suitcase into which she was thrusting whatever came to hand.

"Mum, what are you doing?"

"Packing, Kent, packing as quickly as I can." If the cottage were on fire Maidey could not have reacted more irrationally.

"Are we going away?"

"Yes, yes, as soon as I get everything into this suitcase."

"But, Mum, why? This is our home and Chilham—"

"It's time we left Chilham. We've been here too long as it is."

"Where are we going?"

"I don't know yet, Kent, anywhere, just as long as it's away."

"But your work?"

"I gave my notice."

Kent remembered the letter that had come to his mother yesterday and which she had not read to him. He began to smile uncontrollably. Such excitement possessed him as almost took away any words. He knelt on the floor beside his mother. "Mum, Mum, are we going to Africa to be with Uncle John?"

She drew her hand away from his touch. "Oh, Kent, why must you ask so many questions? Can't you see that I'm pressed? We're going to Margate, or Chatham. Some place where I can get work and you can too. I never want to see Chilham again."

"But we *belong* here, Mum."

She looked at him for the first time since he had come into the room. Her eyes were hard and unseeing, her face white and drawn. "Maybe you do, but I—" Then she put her head in her hands and started to sob.

Kent could not remember ever having seen his mother cry and the sight of her rocking back and forth froze him into a kind of horrified immobility. He wanted to do something for her, he felt there must be something that he could do, but he did not know what it was. Sitting back on the floor, he hugged his arms across his chest for warmth.

Gradually a memory began to work itself up in his mind, something he had utterly forgotten. He had seen his mother cry once before, a long, long time ago, and she had cried in the same way. He must have been sleeping in his crib at the time because he knew that she had picked him up and held him to her. She had sobbed and sobbed, but through her sobs she had kept repeating, "You're all I have now, Kent, all I have." He could feel how his head had rested on her neck, just under her chin, and the quivering feeling of her chin. She had held him so tight he had hardly been able to breathe.

It had frightened him to be held so tight and he could remember the relief he had felt when someone came and took him from her and put him back in his crib. He was cold. His nightshirt was wet and clung to him. He wanted to cry, but he did not. Later, he wondered how much later for then it had seemed as if it must be hours and hours, someone had come and changed his shirt and put him back in his crib.

Kent leaned toward his mother and put his arms around her, holding her with enough strength so that her aimless rocking was checked. "You're all I have, Mum. We belong to each other."

Her damp cheek touched his and Kent realized how hot she was. A new fear gripped him, not with paralysis this time but with action. He had heard enough about the epidemic that had spread through the village during the past fortnight to know that fever went with it, and fever unattended could have serious results.

"Mum," he said earnestly, "I want you to listen to me. I'm going downstairs to get a fire in the grate. As soon as the kettle is boiling I'll put a hot bottle in your bed for you and give you a cup of tea. I want you to get ready for bed. Right now, Mum."

She looked at him, her eyes dulled from weeping, her cheeks red and swollen.

"I'm not asking you to do anything, Mum. I'm telling you what you're going to do."

She nodded numbly.

Kent clattered down the stairs, wishing he had four hands instead of two to accomplish all that he wanted to in as brief a time as possible.

An hour later Maidey was in her bed. The fire was burning busily. The kettle had been at the boil once and a new lot of water was coming up to simmer again. There was the look of warmth in the room though the real feel of it might take longer to come. Maidey, weak and miserable, willingly gave Kent her word that she would not stir from bed while he went to get the doctor.

Kent walked quickly up to the Square, then he ran down the narrow street that led to the doctor's house. Kent had not thought of time and was relieved to hear the bell of St. Mary's telling that the hour was seven o'clock. It should be a good time to find the doctor home. He would probably be having his supper and could come to see the new patient soon.

In answer to Kent's knocking the door was opened, not by the doctor but by his wife. "What is it, boy?" she asked, not recognizing him as he stood on the doorstep.

"I'm Kent," he said, "Kent Conner. My mother and I live in one of the old cottages over at the Lees. She's been taken very ill. Could the doctor come and see her?"

"He's not in just now, Kent. He had a bite of supper an hour ago, then went out again. So many people have been needing him. I'll tell him about your mother when he gets back."

"Will you ask him to come as soon as he can?"

"Indeed I will, and until he gets there do what you can to keep her warm and quiet. Sometimes that's all the doctor can do. And peaceful, that's something the family can do." The telephone could be heard ringing. "She'll be all right, Kent, never fear, and Doctor will be there before long." She closed the door gently.

Kent heard her footsteps on the tile floor, then the phone stopped ringing. He could hear her voice saying almost the same words over again: "—do what you can—yes, I'll tell him."

Kent walked back to the Square. He looked longingly at the signpost, wishing he could follow the arm that pointed westward to the Downs. If Uncle John were only at Beekeep, he could talk with him; he would tell Kent what to do, not just about his mother's sudden illness but about her determination to move away.

He looked at the other arm that pointed eastward to the Lees and followed it. When there was no one around to help, you had to help yourself, Kent told himself, while wondering if all important discoveries had to be made by each person for himself. Passing St. Mary's, he made a gesture of salutation to the fortresslike tower. It had stood strong against the tide of time, holding its own.

When Kent got back to the cottage he found that his mother, half asleep and half awake, was tossing restlessly. He tucked the covers in where they had slipped away, put more coal on the fire, and sat down to await the doctor's call. Sometimes Maidey talked in her sleep as if she were arguing with someone; sometimes she lay very still. Once she opened her eyes wide as if she were quite herself and asked Kent to read to her. He took down from the shelf the book that had been given him by John Rivven and read to her.

"Take of English earth as much
As either hand may rightly clutch.
In the taking of it breathe
Prayer for all who lie beneath—
Not the great nor well bespoke,
But the mere uncounted folk
Of whose life and death is none
Report or lamentation.
Lay that earth upon thy heart,
And thy sickness shall depart!

"It shall sweeten and make whole
Fevered breath and festered soul;
It shall mightily restrain
Over-busy hand and brain;
It shall ease thy mortal strife
'Gainst the immortal woe of life,
Till thyself restored shall prove
By what grace the Heavens do move.

"Take of English flowers these—
Spring's full-faced primroses,
Summer's wild wide-hearted rose,
Autumn's wall-flower of the close,
And, thy darkness to illume,
Winter's bee-thronged ivy bloom.
Seek and serve them where they bide
From Candlemas to Christmas-tide,
For these simples used aright
Can restore a failing sight.

"These shall cleanse and purify
Webbed and inward-turning eye;
These shall show thee treasure hid,
Thy familiar fields amid;
And reveal (which is thy need)
Every man a King indeed!"

"Lay that earth upon thy heart," Maidey murmured, as if she had no voice to say more,"and thy sickness shall depart."

Kent placed the book on the table and stood beside his mother. She seemed to have fallen asleep. When he felt convinced that it was a real sleep and that she was temporarily free of the restless tossing, he took the lamp in his hands and went upstairs to the little room to try to restore it to some semblance of order. He emptied the suitcase and put back into boxes and drawers all the things his mother had filled it with. He picked up and put away as best he could the litter of things on the floor.

Under the suitcase was a small collection of papers, an old newspaper and some letters, and they were the last of the confusion to be accounted for. Not knowing where they belonged, Kent picked up the whole pile and placed them in one of the drawers of the old chest that held his mother's belongings. Someday when she found them there she could restore them to their proper place.

A piece of paper fluttered down to the floor. Kent picked it up and turned it over to see what it was. Small, square and somewhat faded, it was a photograph of a man in uniform, a man with dark hair and a serious quiet expression. Kent studied it closely. There was a hint of a smile about the eyes and the lips looked as if they might part easily with all the things he had to say. The lips—and the sound of the voice that came through them—and the words—Kent listened as he looked. The wonder had not dimmed over the years:

For these simples used aright
Can restore a failing sight.

Kent heard the words, from the past or from within him, it did not matter from whence they came. This was the man who had first given them to him.

These shall show thee treasures hid
Thy familiar fields amid—

Kent held the picture to him, aching with joy and sorrow that he had met his father at last.

His mother was calling him. Slipping the picture into his pocket, he picked up the lamp and went down the stairs. Whether she was calling because she wanted something or because she was talking in a troubled feverish dream, Kent could not tell. She felt hot to his touch and her lips were dry, so he raised her head a little and held some water to her mouth. Maidey took a sip. She opened her eyes wide for a second, then her head went back on the pillow.

"I'll be able to work tomorrow," she said huskily.

Kent laid another chunk of coal on the fire, drew his chair close to it and waited for the doctor. The picture looking down from the mantel where he had propped it made the room seem more like a home. Kent opened Mr. Kipling's book of poems and started to read.

He must have dozed off sometime, for when a tap came at the door Kent woke with a start and could not at first think what it meant. Then, seeing his mother in bed, he realized that the doctor had come at last and went quickly to open the door.

"I'm sorry, Kent, to be so late," the doctor said as he walked past the sleepy-eyed boy to stand beside Maidey Conner.

When he took her pulse and temperature, Maidey opened her eyes to watch him but she made no comment. She closed her eyes again only when the doctor had finally left her bedside.

"Is she very bad, sir?" Kent asked as the doctor stood by the grate for a moment before going out again into the cold.

"Right now, she's uncomfortable but it's nothing for us to worry about. She's got what's been sweeping the countryside this year—high fever and all the evidence of respiratory infection. It won't be serious if you keep her in bed, quiet and warm, until it's run its course."

"Isn't there anything else I can do?"

"I tell most people to keep their patients from worrying, for that's the biggest help of all, but I doubt if I need to tell you that.

Your mother is not the kind of person that I think of as having any worries. Nice-looking man, your father. I knew him well."

Kent smiled with pride that momentarily freed him from anxiety about his mother.

"But there's not much resemblance between you"—the doctor looked from the picture to the boy, comparing the two—"except in the eyes. I wouldn't be surprised if you both looked out on life in the same way. Well, I must be going."

At the door Kent said, "My mother must be worried about something, sir, for when I got home she was packing to go away."

"So!" The doctor raised his brows and drew in his lips. "Fever makes people do strange things."

"She said she'd given her notice."

"Something went wrong in Canterbury, I expect. It often does in those big houses. But it will clear away. Your mother is too valuable a servant for anyone to lose her willingly these days."

"She said she wanted to go away from Chilham," Kent said. Then because he felt that the doctor if anyone would understand he added passionately, "But, sir, we can't go away; we belong here!"

"You do," the doctor said gravely. "A young person's roots go deep in the place where he is born and is growing up, but a woman"—he shook his head—"with her, roots are in the heart and that's a different matter. She can live anywhere if her heart's there."

Kent stared at the doctor uncomprehendingly.

"Get some rest, boy; I'll be in sometime in the morning. I'll send a message to the district nurse to include your mother in her rounds."

During the following week Kent went from home only on brief errands. Everything that had formerly filled his days counted for nothing now. His life consisted in keeping the cottage warm, his mother comfortable, and in giving her the simple food the doctor had suggested. The nurse came in twice a day to care for Maidey in her brusque efficient way. When she left she always made the same remark to Kent: "You can do more for her than anyone, as I would if I could stay. Nursing is more than doctoring when a person's low in mind and body."

Kent wondered if she said it at every cottage. There didn't seem to be anything special that he could do except be there, but that was what Maidey needed. When he went out on his necessary errands he placed the silver nutmeg in her hands to hold onto until his return.

One morning, at the beginning of the second week, Maidey woke from sleep and called to Kent in a quite natural voice.

"What is it, Mum?"

"I'd like a cup of tea, Kent."

He brought it to her and sat on the edge of her bed while she drank it with real enjoyment. Relief surged through Kent that the tide had turned at last and that his mother was on the mend. When he took the empty cup away, she said, "I had such an odd dream last night. It seemed more real that anything present. It was so real it woke me up!"

Kent wondered if she was going to tell it to him.

"I had gone to Beekeep with something to show to Mr. John." She spoke slowly, trying to recall every move, every detail. "Whatever it was I had to show him, I held it cupped in my hands, like this, but I could not show it to him in his sitting room so I took it into the kitchen. When we got there, it was not his kitchen, but mine—this little room where you and I do all our living. Then, when I started to open up my hands to show it to him, I could not see what it was because I was weeping so." Maidey was ready to laugh at herself, part in amusement, part in exasperation. "Fancy me, having a good old cry and in a dream at that!"

It sounded as meaningless to Kent as any dream. The only thing that made it different was that he could not recall his mother ever having told him before of a dream she had had.

"Whatever do you suppose it was that I was holding so carefully in my hands?"

His mother had not really asked him a question she expected him to answer, but Kent felt obliged to make some reply. "Perhaps it was the silver nutmeg."

Maidey moved her head on the pillow. "It was not the souvenir of Ramsgate," she said emphatically. "Why would that make me weep? It was soft; the nutmeg is very hard."

"I don't know," Kent said. Then, because he was the practical man of the house, he went about his duties, cleaning the grate, laying the fire, putting some porridge on to cook, running out to the store for a loaf of bread and six-pennyworth of butter.

After their breakfast together, the first in more than a week, Maidey insisted that Kent go to school. He was loathe to leave her, but she gave him her solemn promise to stay quiet until the doctor came and then to follow his instructions.

"And you'll not think of going away?"

"Whatever do you mean?"

"Packing up, leaving Chilham—"

"When did I ever say that we would do such a thing and where would we go?"

He shrugged his shoulders, but there was no controlling the smile that flashed from his face. How glad he was that he had put everything away in the tumbled room upstairs. It must have been with his mother as the doctor said it was with many people; fever made them do strange things.

With Heart in Hand

9

It was not until after Kent had left for school and the room was still, save for the fire in the grate and the ticking of the clock, that Maidey took eye-stock of her surroundings. Everything looked much as it always did, though she still felt too weak to attempt to raise herself up and really have a good look around.

What she could see, with her head on the pillow, told her that Kent had done as well as a boy could be expected to do and that the room was reasonably tidy. She stared at the calendar on the wall, wondering why it looked so unfamiliar; then she realized that it was because January had been torn from it and the four weeks of February faced her.

Today must be Friday, she reasoned, for when she had persuaded Kent to return to school he had presented her with the argument that it was scarcely worth returning so near the weekend. Her eyes met the date on the calendar. It meant that they were all but through the first week of the new month. She sighed helplessly. There was nothing she could do about that today, she told herself, hoping that by tomorrow she might be able to take hold of things again. A willing prisoner, not only to her promise to Kent but to her own weakness, she relaxed against the comfort of the bed and closed her eyes.

Such utter luxury of rest she remembered feeling only once before in her life and that was the day her baby was born. Blissfully spent from the labor of birth, she had lain back in her bed in the room in the pretty little house on the road to Godmersham. From the window she could see the Downs rolling up to the sky and watch the passing of clouds. She had been filled with marvel that she, Maidey Conner, who had worked as a housemaid since she had left school and until she met and married Lieutenant Conner, USAF, and become a wife, had now become a mother. Between the two experiences lay a year of such happiness as she had never thought to know.

Her husband had secured a week's leave for the time when the baby was due and, contrary to many stories about first births, the baby had arrived on schedule: a boy, sturdy and well formed. Maidey remembered the sound of Kent's footsteps on the stairs when he came up to her room after the doctor had told him the news. He had pushed open the door and stood in the doorway smiling at her, then come into the room softly as if fearful of waking the baby. He had stood by the bed and gazed down at their sleeping son. Maidey could still see the expression on his face when he looked at her, a mixture of pride and love. It did her good to remember it. She began to wonder why for such years she had put those memories away and closed a door in her mind on them all.

She had said one name, looking from father to son, and he had added, "A man of Kent."

Maidey could not recall that she had asked him a question, though she must have, for in another moment he had drawn a chair up to her bed and was explaining to her that a man born east of the Medway River was a man of Kent and west a Kentish man.

"Fancy your knowing more about English ways than I do and I've lived here all my life!"

He had replied that many English customs seemed almost more real to Americans, who knew them only by tradition. They had fallen into talking about the two countries and though Maidey was willing to admit that her son was half American, Kent seemed to prefer to think of him as wholly English.

Maidey, gazing at the new edition of humanity, marveled that small as he was he seemed bigger and more important than either one of his parents or both of them put together. Content to look from one Kent to another and too tired for much talking, she had listened as her husband spoke of the education he wanted for his son and the hopes he had for him. It began to seem as if all the dreams the elder Kent had ever entertained for himself were now lodged in his son. Then the monthly nurse came in to care for the baby. She picked him up from beside his mother and took him into the next room. Kent and Maidey were alone for a while, but it was not the same as it once had been. It would never be the same again. Each one had a new focus, a new point at which their minds met.

Moving slowly in memory through the years, Maidey found that she was able to recall much that had happened during the time they had lived in the house on the Godmersham road. Those were days when she had worked for no one but herself and her own family. She had scrubbed and polished, cooked and cleaned, with a quietness in her heart and a singing pride in all she did. The small Kent had grown and been a joy to them both. Her home was as near as Maidey ever hoped to come on earth to paradise. Kent was often away for several days at a time on training flights. Once he was in America for several weeks. But while he was at Lympne he could get home every night. Sometimes he brought friends of his from the base, but more often they were alone together.

The happiness that was their life had the quality of eternity to it. It had never occurred to Maidey that it could come to an end—that it might, that in time all things did. The day after the baby's fourth birthday, the training plane in which Lieutenant Conner was a passenger crashed on landing. That it could come to an end had apparently been a possibility to Lieutenant Conner, for he had left instructions about his burial in Chilham churchyard. There were other instructions which Maidey was to learn in time, but it was from that point on that the memories began to blur for her.

Kent was gone. She would never see him again or hear his voice. Kent, the man who had been her husband—and that was where the door had begun to swing shut in her mind. Husband no longer, she'd thought bitterly. He's gone.

The door closed on all that had been beautiful and tender during the past four years, closed tight. She wanted not to remember anything about those years. She wanted not to think of them ever again. She locked the door and turned to face the present for what it was and that vast, bleak, unknown area of the future for what it might be. As much as lay within her power, she was determined to destroy the evidence of the years she did not want to remember. She could do it with the household possessions by selling them. She could do it with her son as she kept from him all knowledge of his father. It was a hard way she took for herself, but it seemed the only way in which she could go forward and make any kind of life for herself and her son. Her grief had given way to bitterness.

The house, rented by the month, was soon off her hands and Maidey moved to a small workingman's cottage on the north side of Chilham. Most of the household possessions were sold and the money put in the bank at Canterbury as a lean defense against future needs. She kept only a few things for use in the two rooms that were her present home. She went to Canterbury to look for the only work she knew how to do and was fortunate in finding some. As she could not leave the four-year-old boy alone, she brought him along with her and found a woman in straits like herself who was willing to board him during the day for a small sum.

"He's a bonny lad," the woman had said, "and who might his father be?"

"An air force man," Maidey answered, "nobody in particular and dead these past three weeks."

The woman had raised her eyes and smiled understandingly. Kent, who picked up words like a parrot, caught on to one his mother had used.

"Nobody, nobody," he sang out, proud of what he considered as a surname, which he knew only as a pleasing sound. "Me, I'm nobody."

Maidey paid the woman her few shillings for the week in advance and went out to the kitchen work which would bring her enough to pay their rent and buy their food. The clothes she wore and those she possessed would last her well; the baby would need little more than he already had for the next year or two.

She could see that the future for her would hold hard work and long hours, one free day a week and a week with pay in the summer. It would hold, as well, a growing boy with a constant need for good food and, once he started in at school, for clothes and shoes. The boy could leave school when he was sixteen and go to work. Twelve years until that time.

Maidey was thirty years old. She came of strong stock though her parents had died when she was young. There was nothing that could happen to her, she convinced herself, barring some misfortune, that could keep her from work until the boy was able to take care of himself. In spite of all that his father had once said about an education, this was the way things were now and the way they would have to be.

She bolted the door on the past and set her face to all the future she could see; she felt safe within the framework she had devised.

* * *

The doctor came in at midmorning and pronounced Maidey on the road to recovery.

"When may I get up?"

"Not today, Mrs. Conner, and not tomorrow, but the day after you may have your tea sitting in a chair by the fire. The next day you may move around your home as much as you like, and the next"—he held up his hand and counted off four fingers—"that will be the fifth day from now, if it is fine you may go out."

Maidey smiled weakly. There seemed a great deal to remember; even looking ahead so many days was an effort.

The doctor, as if aware of her thoughts, said sympathetically, "Don't worry, Mrs. Conner, the way you feel now is no gauge to the way you'll feel tomorrow. You've had a big battle, but you've won. Once your strength comes back it will be like the incoming tide. You won't be able to stop it. That is, if you don't strain the little strength you have now."

"But my work?"

"Never you mind, Mrs. Conner, there's always work for someone like you and another place will be available as good if not better than your last. And, Mrs. Conner, if you've any need in the meantime, there's more than one person, including my wife and myself, who would be glad to carry you over."

"Thank you, Doctor," Maidey said, "but I've enough to take care of myself and the boy until I can work again."

At the door the doctor turned back to look at Maidey. "He's a fine boy, that son of yours. I shouldn't be surprised to see him make his mark in the world one day."

At noon the nurse came in and made Maidey comfortable. She built up the fire, changed the sheets on the bed, and prepared some luncheon. She propped up the pillows so Maidey could sit up. "You see a deal more when you sit than when you're lying down," she said.

After she left, Maidey wondered what she meant. True, she could see the fire now instead of the light from it flickering on the ceiling. She could watch flames curling around the new chunks of coal that had been placed on the bed of embers. The sight of them made her feel warm. She could see, as well, the walls stained by damp and the worn carpet, the chair that should be recovered if they ever had a visitor, and on the table the book that Mr. Rivven had given to Kent.

She could see, too, how neatly Kent had kept the place during the time of her illness. Even her trained eye could not discover dust on the surfaces or fluff on the floor. The brass coal scuttle needed polishing, but she could hardly expect Kent to have thought of that. Everything looked as it should, as it always had.

Maidey's eyes rested on the mantel, held by the small photograph that had been set there. It was a face that she had not seen for years, a clean and pleasant face. Looking at it, she wondered now why it was that she had kept him out of her life for so long. It seemed so right to have him in it again. Kent must have found the picture

somewhere and placed it there. She did not resent his doing so. The man in uniform belonged to them both.

It did not seem difficult now, as she looked at him, to think back to the days when they had been husband and wife. While it lasted it had been good. Everything must come to end sometime, even the experience of love. She could remember the way they had met, the day they had married, the week they had spent in London, the summer holiday at Ramsgate when he had bought her the silver nutmeg. She could remember that her only fear in those days had been not that he might meet with any mishap, but that he might want her to go to America with him.

America was so big, so distant, so totally unknown, and she did not want to go there. Chilham was tidy and small and familiar, and she did not want to leave it. He promised her that she would never have to go to America, that she was England to him and must remain so. She knew that he might have to go to America from time to time, but that he would return to her and to Chilham.

He spoke often to her of the work he wanted to do, of the books he hoped to write, and how she could help him best by doing what she did best, taking care of the house and keeping things peaceful for him. "Quiet and peaceful" were the words he used so frequently, as if he found their meaning in her company, as if that was all he ever wanted; but she knew that a man needed good food as well and she was happy that she could give him what he needed. If he had lived, she caught her breath, if he had lived—

Looking at his picture on the mantel had brought him into her life again. It seemed good to think of him without bitterness, to see him take a place in her home. And it was good to remember love and the ways of love, the white radiance that took possession of one's being when one knew, as she had once, that beyond any question to love was enough. To love whether it was sought, whether it was returned, was enough; but with Kent it had been sought, it had been returned. It had ended, as all things mortal must.

Now, after seven lonely years, she found that she could begin to think of such things again. The grief and bitterness within her had gone and in their place was only the remembrance of something that had once been beautiful and that had been hers alone. Her mind had gone back the long journey of the years; now it made a shorter journey of the weeks. Why had she felt so afraid at that stirring within her heart, that quickening? Why had she wanted to run away from everything she knew?

She reached under her pillow for the silver nutmeg and turned it in her hands. It was a pretty thing. She shook it and the earth within it gave a small rattling sound. No, this was not what she had cupped in her hands in the dream. The silver nutmeg belonged to the past. The other held the future in its embrace as the nutmeg held the granules of earth. Then Maidey made a clicking sound with her tongue against her teeth, surprised at herself and not a little exasperated that the dawn stealing over her had taken so long to make itself felt.

Now that it had come, she saw completely and reasonably that what she had been holding in the dream had been her heart. She had hidden it in her clumsy, work-roughened hands and wept. She had gone with it from one room to another because she could reveal it only in her own homely and familiar surroundings. Maidey gave a sigh of relief and smiled up at the picture looking down on her from the mantel. Kent's hand could be heard on the latch of the door. Maidey slid the nutmeg under her pillow and turned to face him as he came into the room.

Return of the Herons

10

During the next few days Maidey did exactly as the doctor had told her to do. She sat in a chair by the fire on the first day out of bed, busying her hands in cutting out red hearts and gray feathers for the St. Valentine's Day party that Kent was helping to prepare at school. On the second day she moved around her small house, even going to the upstairs room to see how it looked. She had had a bothersome feeling that it was in need of a straightening, but it seemed to look as it should, as it always did, and Kent had made his bed neatly before he had gone to school. Relieved, Maidey went downstairs and sat by the fire to rest.

There was a book lying on the table and she picked it up. It opened easily, and Maidey found herself reading the familiar verses with more than her eyes.

. . . sweeten and make whole
Fevered breath and festered soul;
It shall mightily restrain
Over-busy hand and brain;
. . . thyself restored shall prove
By what grace the Heavens do move.

Reading awhile, then closing her eyes and dreaming of things that had been and things that might be, she felt that at last she had come face to face with herself again after many years.

It was so that the doctor found her when he called in the late afternoon. He made his brief examination and pronounced everything normal.

"Pulse, temperature, are good and right." He smiled proudly at her. "Wish I could see everyone make the kind of recovery you are making, Mrs. Conner."

"Thank you, Doctor."

"But, easy does it for another few days," he cautioned, "and I don't want you to go out just yet. The sun has been getting warmer but the air is still raw."

"Very good," Maidey said. There was nothing in particular that she wanted to go out for and she found it not difficult to yield to the doctor's wishes. "How soon may I work around my own house?"

"The day after tomorrow you may do anything you want, and the day after that you may go out for a bit, if it's fine."

Maidey repeated his last words, relishing the familiar ring.

"Good day, Mrs. Conner. I have no excuse now to come and see you again."

"I'm very grateful to you, Doctor."

* * *

Kent insisted on waiting on his mother for one more evening, getting their tea, tending the fire, and seeing to it that everything was in order for the next day. Maidey submitted to him because it was for the last time. She could feel her own strength returning as the hours went on.

The energy that surged within her was put to good use the next morning after Kent had left for school. In spite of his care of the cottage, she could see as soon as she began to move around that it had lacked a woman's touch. There was washing to do of the small things that could dry on a rack by the fire, and then there was ironing; there was cleaning and polishing. She took stock of her food cupboard and made a list for Kent when he went up to the store.

She moved peacefully from one self-imposed task to another, knowing that she had the whole day before her and there were no demands of any kind on her time. She rested frequently, and cosied herself with more than one cup of tea. She looked over Kent's clothes and discovered that his better jacket was beginning to wear thin at the elbows.

When Kent returned from school it was to see his mother sitting by the fire, his jacket on her lap, weaving a needle and thread in and out of the cloth. She looked so quiet and peaceful that Kent stood in the doorway to fill his eyes with the good sight of her. He decided then that she even looked beautiful. He had never thought that of his mother before, except perhaps on the day she had cooked the Christmas dinner at Beekeep and they had all been so happy. He closed the door behind him and crossed the room to stand beside her.

"Mum, I like to come in from school and find you here. I wish you didn't have to go to work ever again."

"And when would you have a new jacket if I didn't work?" Maidey held up the one she was repairing. "I want to have this one fit for you to wear to your party at school tomorrow."

"It really won't matter, Mum, how I look. There's going to be games and stories, and something special to eat. Oh, Mum, the room does look beautiful! Tessa and I have just been helping Miss Hinshaw decorate it with all those hearts and feathers you helped me make. It's going to be a real celebration."

"All the more reason for you to look nice for it."

"Mum, no one is going to have time to look at anyone's clothes."

"Even so, I want you to look your best, or at least as well as you can until I can get out to buy you something new. You're growing so, Kent! It's not just wear that's putting a strain on woolen."

Maidey hummed happily as she wove her thread back and forth. "Your father was always so particular about his uniforms. I used to keep them pressed just so for him, and I polished his buttons every night. In those days nothing stood between him and getting a new uniform if he had the mind." Maidey held the jacket up and shook it. "Whatever's that?"

A feather floated gently down to lie on the floor between them.

Kent reached to pick it up. "It's a heron's feather. I found it yesterday on the Downs." He moved it across his cheek, then brushed it over his mother's forehead. "It's a sign that the herons will soon return and all will be well for another year." Kent placed the feather on the mantel beside the picture of his father.

"Your father used to make up stories to tell you when you were a little boy. I never thought you'd be making them up to tell me."

"Some of them are true, Mum."

"You're so sure, Kent, about those birds. I don't know how it is you can be."

Kent, if he heard her, did not reply. Instead he asked her the question that had been aching within him ever since the picture of his father had taken its place on the mantel. "Mum, do you think my father would have been a little like Uncle John if he lived?"

Maidey caught her breath—say one thing and it might close forever the door that had been slowly opening; say another and it might hold the door open. She said the other, not with words but by nodding her head.

That night, long after Kent had gone upstairs to bed, Maidey sat by the fire. Handwork had been put aside, as well as reading. The lamp was turned low and her chair was drawn close to the grate. She had much to think about as she stared into the fire, and much to see. Once, when a chunk of coal broke and thin flames licked up the two shining black sides, Maidey felt that she could see the future opening before her. Think about Kent and his father as much as she liked, think about Mr. John as much as she dared, she kept coming back to thoughts of herself. She could not say now that life for her was with other people, but she knew now that life for her was in the work of her hands for those she loved.

New warmth glowed from the fire as the coal burned and snapped. She held her hands to it hungrily. A great relief came over her as she realized that she had freed herself at last to love again. How was it she could have thought that love was mortal and would die as all things mortal must? she asked herself. Love could not die.

That was what the heron said, or was it? She smiled. She was beginning to sound like the artist himself!

After a while, Maidey took from the drawer in the table a pad and pencil. She wrote a few lines, read them carefully to herself in the dim lamplight, then folded the paper into an envelope. She wrote the address with the same care, then placed a stamp on the envelope and sealed it with quiet deliberateness. She got up and slipped her coat on and went out into the night.

Without stopping to take any stock of the outer world from which she had been kept for so many days, she walked up to the Square, crossed the end that was opposite the castle gates, then went down the narrow street to the post office. Once there, she deposited her letter in the pillar box in the wall. She turned away quickly and walked back to the Square. There she stood still, breathing the sharp night air and looking around her.

The Square was deserted. There was not a light to be seen in any of the houses, but there were stars in the sky. Maidey gave a little gasp at the sight of them. She had been housed so long that she had almost forgotten how bright the sky could be with stars.

"It will be fine tomorrow!" she exclaimed inwardly, as if surprised at something she had not expected quite so soon.

The wind that whipped by her came over the Downs from the northwest, the quarter of good weather. She could no more hold back that wind and the slow turning of the earth that would bring the morning sun to Chilham than she could the delivery of the letter she had entrusted to Her Majesty's Mail. Maidey walked home slowly. It was her first time out in so long that she felt she could not breathe enough of the night air which, sharp as it was, was nourishing. She knew that she had gone outdoors a few hours earlier than the doctor had given her leave, but who would ever know and what harm could it do? Strength was a surging tide within her and something close kin to joy rode upon its crest.

Kent left early for school in a flurry of excitement about the party. He had not wanted to wear a sweater under his coat, but Maidey had insisted.

"The sun may be shining now, Kent, but there's little warmth in it yet and who's to say what the weather may be doing when you're on your way home? And Kent, mind that you be back in time for tea today."

Kent said yes about the tea and agreed to wear the sweater. He could not help but laugh at the swift turn events had taken. His mother had been doing what he had told her to do for days and days; it was only fair that he should yield now to her wishes.

Maidey stood in the door and watched him as he went up the hill by the old church. He used to walk the long way by the Downs; she was glad that he had taken to going the shorter way. "We all have our reasons for the things we do," Maidey murmured compassionately as she turned and went inside.

She had plenty to do to keep herself occupied until early afternoon. She had not made a cake for a long time but when it came from the oven she was glad to see that her hand had lost none of its skill. While it was cooling she laid the table for tea with a cloth that had to be pressed to free it from the folds that had deepened from lying unused in a drawer. Her best tea set, taken from the box in which it had spent most of the last seven years, had to be washed before it could be placed on the table. Three cups and saucers, three plates, three of everything, she saw with satisfaction on the table.

By midafternoon Maidey could see nothing more to do and because the day remained sunny and there was still better than an hour before tea, she went for a walk. The Square was almost as deserted as it had been the previous midnight. Maidey saw that snowdrops were still blooming in some of the cottage gardens and crocuses were opening their cups. The air was quick with the twittering of birds.

Reaching the church she stopped on the steps to look around her, then went up to the door that would always open at the push of a hand and went inside. Reverence had taken such possession of her that she felt a momentary need for churchly quiet. She had prayed long enough that she would know the right thing to do. Now she could only do what her heart told her. The cold within the thick-walled church soon crept up on her and she shivered. Later, when she went out into the sunshine, the day seemed to have a summerlike warmth.

Looking up at the clock face on the square tower of the church, she saw the position of the gold hands in relation to her next duty. That was how she had always seen a clock for as long as she could remember: time with respect to the task a particular hour required. Today was no different. She gazed at the clock as if it were the face of her employer. And yet today was different. So often the task or duty was performed for someone in whom she had no particular interest, except that the work be done well enough to justify her wages. Now those great hands, moving slowly but inexorably, said that her next task would be done in her own home for those she loved. They said also that there was time for the walk she wanted to take.

Maidey put the sun at her back and went into the old graveyard, past the ancient stones with their worn inscriptions, past the great yews that had stood there for a thousand years, growing thicker and darker so that night seemed to be held forever in their branches. She crossed the road and went into the new part of the graveyard, toward the stone that had weathered little in the time it had stood there. She laid her hand on it, surprised at the warmth it had caught from the sun, and was giving to her; surprised, as she always was, at kindliness directed toward her.

* * *

Kent willingly walked home with Tessa the long way by the Downs. They had much to talk over about their St. Valentine's Day party and Kent thought to continue on the extra distance to Beekeep to see if it showed signs of life within it. They fell silent as they came up over the rise where the first view opened before them. Misty shafts of late-afternoon sunshine lay over the land, shifting, catching bright on the outcropping chalk cliffs, losing themselves in the blue shadows that rested in the folds of the hills. Here and there the river flashed back the light as if returning signals to the sky. By common consent they stood still for a moment to let their gaze travel down the landscape, across the fields, some of them bright green, others dark brown with the plowed earth waiting for the spring planting.

It was Tessa who realized first that somebody else was also standing still. She drew in her breath and laid her hand on Kent's arm. Five somebodies were standing in the field below them.

"They've come back! The herons have come back!" she whispered.

"And on the very day, St. Valentine's Day!" Kent breathed, his voice low with wonder at what they were seeing.

The herons were standing still as if they were made of any substance but sensitive flesh, hollow bones, and gray-blue feathers. All were facing the same way, their necks drawn in, their long-beaked heads sunk into their shoulders. They did not stir even when another bird came down from the sky with wide-open wings, spiraling, banking, then alighting at the end of the line. He steadied himself for a moment, then with a curious gait, half run, half skip, went down the line to take his place at the other end. As if summoned to life, the standing herons flapped their wings, took a few steps forward and back, then lapsed again into their silent stance.

Without sound or warning, one of the first five unfolded its wings, unlimbered its long legs, took a few running steps forward and gained the air, flapping leisurely, rising higher and heading toward Felborough Wood where the heronry was. Kent watched the wide turn in the air, then the swift zigzagging descent as the bird approached the treetops. He could not see the bird alight, but he knew that it had as it disappeared among the trees.

"Safe!" Tessa exclaimed.

"Perhaps in his very own nest where he was a chick last summer."

Now there were a dozen birds on the field and they were no longer standing still.

"Look," Kent said, hard put to keep his voice low in his excitement, "they're dancing!"

Reaching out their necks they grasped each others' beaks and moved stiffly forward and back, forward and back. Then, seized by a common impulse, they stretched out their wings, ran ahead on their stiff ungainly legs and took off from the gathering ground for the sky; but not now in search of any aerial highway, only the shortest way to their nests. They made a sweep in the sky, passing over the village, before they set their course for the heronry.

Tessa and Kent waited for a few moments, but no more birds came. They faced each other. There seemed to be no available words, even for two who had achieved the high mark in school composition, to say what they were feeling at what they had witnessed, or what they knew it signified. By mutual, though silent, consent they parted, Tessa to start running the short distance to her home, Kent to go on his way. Mindful of his promise to his mother to be home in time for tea, he deferred his walk to Beekeep and turned back toward Chilham; but he found it hard to leave, though the field where the herons had gathered was empty and the sky revealed no lofty flyers.

Before the path started to go downhill, he stopped once again, stood still, and scanned the wide landscape. A man was coming along the path some distance behind him. At sight of Kent, his voice rolled cheerfully on the air.

Suddenly it seemed to Kent as if time had folded itself up into something so small that it would have lost itself if he had put it in his pocket. He shouted a greeting, then ran to shorten the distance. Once he felt the embrace of familiar arms, Kent knew that time had vanished utterly. Uncle John might never have been away at all. It was so natural to be together again.

"When did you get back?"

"Yesterday, about midday. I made it just in time."

"You did, Uncle John, you did!"

"They've been coming in all day, landing in that lower field, standing still as judges, then talking to each other now and again about all the things the birds at this time of the year talk about. There'll probably be another flight in before sunset."

Kent gazed in surprise at the two arms swinging free, no artist's equipment under one, no tea basket held in the other.

"Hungry?"

Kent nodded. "I expect it is getting on toward tea time."

"Expect?" John Rivven laughed. "You jolly well know it is and we'll have it together, but not sitting on a log or at Beekeep. Your mother asked me to have tea with you both on the next fine day. Wouldn't you say this is it?"

Kent glanced overhead as if for the first time he was taking the quality of the day into consideration, and just then he saw the new arrivals coming in with steady sweep of wings and long, outstretched necks. Even their crested heads could be seen and their wind-ruffled breast feathers as they rode the sky with proud and leisured assurance.

"Look!" Kent shouted.

"I am."

Together they stood as still as the birds would once they had landed.

High and circling wide, then narrowing their circle so that it no longer included village square and castle grounds but only the gathering field, the wild, light slender birds seemed to float and waver in the air, but always they were going each one like an arrow shot by an archer whose direction was sure. One at a time they landed in the field, drew their necks in, hunched their wings, and settled into their silent time of rest which preceded the last mile to their nests.

"How do they know," Kent breathed, "how do they know exactly what to do and where to go? How do they know?"

"There are some things of which every one of us can be sure," John Rivven murmured, "some things."

* * *

Maidey had seen them when she was standing by the white stone in the new churchyard. Deep in her thoughts, she had not known what it was at first when she heard a sound like wind in the trees nearby but felt not the slightest movement of air on her face. She had looked up to see where the wind could be, and then she had seen the great birds—five—six—seven of them, flying just above the treetops in a wide circle as they passed over the village. She could see them clearly, and now they were not bird only but welcome symbol. She breathed in until the cold air choked her. So they had come back, and all would be well for another year!

She found herself repeating the saying that was rooted deep in the heart of her countryside. If all would be well with the village it would be well with her, and love would come again for her no less than for the herons. All would be well. That was what the returning birds were saying, and the round of the year as it moved from winter into spring.

The striking of the bell from the church tower had only one meaning for Maidey. She lifted her hand from the white stone and started in the direction of her home, running a few steps every now and then. Birds might fly in the sky as they always had, but she had work to do. A man and a boy were coming to tea and she must be home in time to have it ready for them.